P9-DSY-588

USA TODAY'S DEBATE: VOICES AND PERSPECTIVES

INTERNET CENSORSHIP

Protecting Citizens or Trampling Freedom?

Christine Zuchora-Walske

FOR RON, TONY, AND MARIA

USA TODAY®, its logo, and associated graphics are federally registered trademarks. All rights are reserved. All USA TODAY text, graphics and photographs are used pursuant to a license and may not be reproduced, distributed or otherwise used without the express written consent of Gannett Co., Inc.

USA TODAY Snapshots®, graphics, and excerpts from USA TODAY articles quoted on back cover and on pages 10–11, 12, 38–39, 40, 48–49, 54–55, 56–57, 59, 63, 65, 67, 70–71, 72, 74–75, 81, 84, 86–87, 93, 98–99, 102, 116–117, 120, 127 © copyright 2010 by USA TODAY.

Text copyright © 2010 by Lerner Publishing Group, Inc.

All rights reserved. International copyright secured. No part of this book may be reproduced, stored in a retrieval system, or transmitted in any form or by any means—electronic, mechanical, photocopying, recording, or otherwise—without the prior written permission of Lerner Publishing Group, Inc., except for the inclusion of brief quotations in an acknowledged review.

Twenty-First Century Books
A division of Lerner Publishing Group, Inc.
241 First Avenue North
Minneapolis, MN 55401 U.S.A.

Website address: www.lernerbooks.com

The publisher wishes to thank Ben Nussbaum and Phil Pruitt of USA TODAY for their help in preparing this book.

Library of Congress Cataloging-in-Publication Data

Zuchora-Walske, Christine.
    Internet censorship : protecting citizens or trampling freedom? / by Christine Zuchora-Walske.
        p.   cm. — (USA today's debate : voices and perspectives)
    Includes bibliographical references and index.
    ISBN 978-0-7613-5118-4 (lib. bdg. : alk. paper)
    1. Internet—Access control—United States. 2. Internet—Censorship—United States.
    3. Internet—Government policy—United States. 4. Censorship—United States. I. Title.
    TK5105.875.I57Z93 2010
    005.8—dc22   2009050921

Manufactured in the United States of America
1 – DP – 12/15/09

CONTENTS

INTRODUCTION
The Internet Censorship
Debate. 5

CHAPTER ONE
U.S. Censorship History. 15

CHAPTER TWO
Censorship in the
Internet Age 43

CHAPTER THREE
Child Safety. 61

CHAPTER FOUR
Public Morality. 77

CHAPTER FIVE
Security 91

CHAPTER SIX
Intellectual Property. . 105

EPILOGUE
The Future of
Online Freedom. 129

Timeline 136
Glossary. 140
Source Notes. 142
Selected Bibliography. 148
Organizations to Contact. . . . 150
Further Information 153
Index. 156

myspace.com.

a place for friends

Home | Browse | Search

Cool New Videos

The Ice
Breaker

Jason

Hank
Ketchum

Millionares

Introduction

The Internet Censorship Debate

IN LATE SUMMER 2006, THIRTEEN-YEAR-OLD MEGAN Meier of Dardenne Prairie, Missouri, opened an account on the social networking website MySpace. She soon made a new cyberfriend named Josh Evans. Evans said he was sixteen years old. He explained that he'd just moved with his mom and two brothers to O'Fallon, a nearby town.

Over the next six weeks, Megan and Josh got acquainted. Megan seemed happier than she'd been in a long time. She had struggled with attention deficit disorder, depression, and weight issues. She had been seeing a therapist for a few years. But after switching schools, losing 20 pounds (9 kilograms), and moving on from old friendships to new ones, Megan was feeling optimistic.

On October 15, 2006, Megan got an unsettling message from Josh. It read, "I don't know if I want to be friends with you anymore because I've heard that you are not very nice to your friends." Megan was confused

Left: The Internet allows people to share more information than ever before. But it also allows people to share harmful or false information easily.

and frantic. She fired off a reply, asking Josh what he was talking about.

The next day, Megan logged on to MySpace to see if Josh had responded. She wanted to know why his behavior toward her had changed so suddenly.

Josh had indeed responded— and his messages were getting meaner. Among other things, he said, "Everybody in O'Fallon knows how you are. You are a bad person and everybody hates you.... The world would be a better place without you."

Megan sent Josh one last message. "You are the kind of boy a girl would kill herself over," she wrote. Then she hung herself with a belt in her bedroom closet. She died the next day.

Six weeks later, Megan's parents discovered that Josh Evans didn't exist. "Josh" was actually Lori Drew, an adult neighbor. Drew's daughter and Megan had been friends, but Megan had recently ended the friendship. Drew had joined MySpace to find out what Megan was saying about her daughter online. According to a neighbor in whom Drew had confided, Drew had wanted to "mess with

Lori Drew *(center)* and her daughter *(left)* arrive at federal court in Los Angeles, where Lori faced charges of cyberbullying.

Megan"—gain her trust, then dash it. Drew had known that Megan suffered from depression.

Police investigated the incident. Drew stood trial in federal court and was initially convicted of misdemeanors (minor crimes). But the judge later threw out those convictions, finding that Drew had not actually broken any laws.

Americans were furious over Drew's lack of punishment for tormenting Megan. Public outrage over this and other similar incidents inspired many new local and state laws.

By 2009 thirteen states had passed laws to curb cyberbullying, and several other states were considering such laws. Cyberbullying is harassing a child (anyone seventeen years or younger) electronically, such as through the Internet or by cell phone.

Most of the state laws require schools to develop rules about cyberbullying. Some go further. For example, under a 2008 Missouri act, cyberbullies who are twenty-one years or older face felony (serious crime) charges and up to four years in prison.

At the federal (national government) level, U.S. representative Linda Sanchez introduced the Megan Meier Cyberbullying Prevention Act in 2008 and again in 2009. The key provision in this bill, often called simply House Resolution (HR) 1966, says:

> Whoever transmits in interstate or foreign commerce

Above: Megan's mother, Tina Meier, holds pictures of her daughter. Tina has become a crusader against cyberbullying.

any communication, with the intent to coerce [force], intimidate, harass, or cause substantial emotional distress to a person, using electronic means to support severe, repeated, and hostile behavior, shall be fined under this title or imprisoned not more than two years, or both.

SAFEGUARD OR CENSORSHIP?

Supporters of cyberbullying laws say these measures are necessary to protect kids' mental and physical health. Bullying is not just child's play, they say. It presents serious dangers not only to victims but also to communities.

Sanchez explained, "A young person exposed to repeated, severe and hostile bullying online is deserving of protections because bullying puts them at risk for depression and suicide." In addition, she cited a U.S. Secret Service study that suggested that children who are bullied might later commit violence at school.

Supporters note that U.S. laws forbid bullying behavior when it happens in person. For example, stalking and sexual harassment are illegal. And the U.S. Supreme Court has ruled many times that words can be dangerous. According to the Court, when words present a grave risk of harm, regulating them is appropriate. Sanchez says that cyberbullying laws "give judges and juries discretion to recognize the difference between an annoying chain email, a righteously angry political blog post, or a miffed text to an ex-boyfriend and serious,

" Free speech does not involve speech directed at someone to intimidate, frighten, or otherwise harass them. "

—MISSOURI LAWYER JACK BANAS, 2009

> " **Freedom of speech has certain limitations . . . but the Framers of the Constitution wanted the role of government very circumscribed [limited] when dealing with what people say.** "
>
> —MISSOURI BLOGGER TIMOTHY BIRDNOW, 2009

repeated, hostile communications made with the intent to harm."

Critics, on the other hand, worry that such laws trample Americans' cherished free-speech rights. Missouri lawyer Michael Kielty believes HR 1966 is too general and too vague. "It's a terribly crafted statute [law]," he says. It states that an adult who causes emotional distress in a child via electronic communication is a felon. "Can you imagine the application of that in everyday life? With your children? With teachers and students? It is a slippery slope [will lead to unintended consequences]."

Many Americans feel the same way about HR 1966. Jacqui Cheng, an editor at the technology news website Ars Technica, says, "The language in the bill is so vague, it could be interpreted to apply to practically any situation, including blog posts critical of public officials."

Others believe HR 1966 violates the U.S. Constitution. Missouri blogger Timothy Birdnow insists, "There is no right in the Constitution to be free of verbal mistreatment from another citizen. . . . Yes, freedom of speech has certain limitations . . . but the Framers of the Constitution wanted the role of government very circumscribed [limited] when dealing with what people say." Birdnow and other critics recognize the noble intent behind cyberbullying laws but warn that "noble purposes have been corrupted many times in the past."

States push for cyberbully controls

From the Pages of
USA TODAY

The problem of cyberbullying gained national attention last November when the story surfaced of a 13-year-old Missouri girl who killed herself following an Internet hoax.

The death of Megan Meier, who was allegedly tormented by a neighbor on the Web, echoed another case three years earlier in Vermont. There, a 13-year-old boy committed suicide after being bullied online by peers who spread rumors that he was gay.

Those incidents—along with an increasing number of complaints from teenagers, parents and educators—are spurring state lawmakers across the USA to draft legislation giving schools more power to do something about bullying over the Internet.

At least seven states, including Iowa, Minnesota, New Jersey and Oregon, passed cyberbullying laws in 2007. Five more—Maryland, Missouri, New York, Rhode Island and Vermont—are considering similar legislation this year.

Most of the laws are confined to the use of school computers or networks. Others, such as those passed in Arkansas and Delaware, call for education officials to take action against off-campus bullying that disrupts their schools.

In New Jersey, some school districts, taking a cue from state officials, are considering policies that assert their authority outside of school. Such policies are raising concerns about infringing on freedom of speech and intruding into students' private lives.

"The lines between home and school are continuing to blur with more expectations for schools to exercise authority in areas previously reserved for parents," said Max Riley, superintendent of the Randolph School District in New Jersey.

After New Jersey passed a law last year requiring schools to ban cyberbullying, the state Department of Education issued guidelines. School administrators were told they "may impose consequences" for off-campus bullying—but only when it "substantially interferes" with a school's operation.

Riley said the Randolph district had been considering a policy used in other districts that goes further than the state statute by stating school officials "will impose consequences" on certain acts of off-campus bullying. Randolph's finished policy will exclude references to off-campus behavior, Riley said.

"I am leery of going too far and trying to regulate too much of private life, even though I abhor some of the things that kids put up on the Internet about each other," Riley said.

The American Civil Liberties Union has opposed some cyberbullying laws, saying they set up school officials to trample on students' First Amendment [constitutional] rights. The ACLU helped block a proposal last year to expand an Oregon law to include off-campus bullying, arguing that school officials have no right to impose punishment on students for what they do away from school.

"That doesn't mean a school district can't be involved," said David Fidanque, executive director of the ACLU of Oregon. "The most important thing is to notify a parent. Most cyberbullying outside of school involves mean, insensitive statements posted on somebody's Facebook page. There's no real threat and no real impact other than hurt feelings."

Nancy Willard, executive director of the Center for Safe and Responsible Internet Use in Oregon, lobbied unsuccessfully to expand the law, saying most bullying takes place on home computers. She said Internet bullying is especially harmful because cyberbullies have such a large audience. "The off-campus acts are far more harmful, and the impact is coming to the schools," she said.

Megan Meier's suicide in Missouri prompted Gov. Matt Blunt to create an Internet Harassment Task Force. Last month, the task force proposed making it a crime to harass someone over the Internet. It also called on state education officials to create computer ethics classes.

New cyberbullying laws could lead to freedom-of-speech challenges, according to Vito Gagliardi, a New Jersey attorney who represents school districts.

"Someone might say it's my opinion so-and-so is a nerd and the First Amendment [of the Constitution] allows me to say that," Gagliardi said.

—Abbott Koloff

Some people have taken to calling HR 1966 "the Censorship Act." Censorship is suppressing (forbidding, silencing, or punishing) communications. Most Americans—whatever they may think about HR 1966—oppose censorship. It denies one of their most prized and basic rights: freedom of speech.

THE LARGER DEBATE

Are cyberbullying laws a form of censorship? What about other laws that affect electronic communications?

Americans are sharply divided on the issue of Internet censorship. Free speech and censorship work side by side in U.S. society. Both aim to protect the public. Americans struggle over the best way to balance them.

Some people believe that censoring online material is the best way to achieve or preserve certain important public goals. These goals include child safety, national security, and creativity.

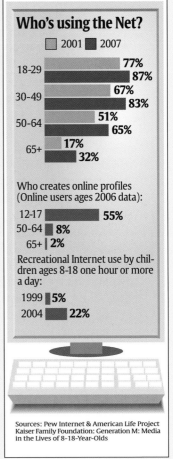

Who's using the Net?

☐ 2001 ■ 2007

18-29 — 77% / 87%
30-49 — 67% / 83%
50-64 — 51% / 65%
65+ — 17% / 32%

Who creates online profiles (Online users ages 2006 data):

12-17 — 55%
50-64 — 8%
65+ — 2%

Recreational Internet use by children ages 8-18 one hour or more a day:

1999 — 5%
2004 — 22%

Sources: Pew Internet & American Life Project Kaiser Family Foundation: Generation M: Media in the Lives of 8-18-Year-Olds

By Robert W. Ahrens, USA TODAY, 2007

Other people strongly disagree. They believe that to govern themselves well, Americans must be able to share ideas—even offensive or controversial ones—freely. They insist that censorship is rarely the best way to achieve any positive goal.

The Internet censorship debate is complicated. It is made up of several smaller debates and involves many sticky questions:

What's the best way to keep children safe online? Should we use laws to protect children from inappropriate online content?

Is a combination of education and parental involvement a better strategy?

Is it possible—or even desirable—to demand civility (polite behavior) on the Internet? Does online civility help preserve a peaceful society? Should Internet users adhere to traditional customs and morals (rules about right and wrong), or do such rules squash the free exchange of ideas, a key element of democracy?

Can national security and online privacy coexist? Should the government be allowed to investigate and monitor the online behavior of suspected terrorists? Should Americans be willing to trade their privacy for a potentially safer country?

How can U.S. society protect creative works from online piracy? Should we use strict laws and electronic "locks" to prevent the unauthorized transmission of online artwork, music, and writing? Or do these tools chill free expression and invade privacy?

To answer these and other questions about Internet censorship, we must look at censorship throughout U.S. history. We must investigate how Internet censorship can benefit and harm U.S. society. We must also examine law and public opinion concerning online speech. Only then can we make our own informed opinions.

IN CONGRESS, JULY 4, 1776.

The unanimous Declaration of the thirteen united States of America

When in the Course of human events, it becomes necessary for one people to dissolve the political bands which have connected them with another, and to assume among the powers of the earth, the separate and equal station to which the Laws of Nature and of Nature's God entitle them, a decent respect to the opinions of mankind requires that they should declare the causes which impel them to the separation. — We hold these truths to be self-evident, that all men are created equal, that they are endowed by their Creator with certain unalienable Rights, that among these are Life, Liberty and the pursuit of Happiness. — That to secure these rights, Governments are instituted among Men, deriving their just powers from the consent of the governed, — That whenever any Form of Government becomes destructive of these ends, it is the Right of the People to alter or to abolish it, and to institute new Government, laying its foundation on such principles and organizing its powers in such form, as to them shall seem most likely to effect their Safety and Happiness. Prudence, indeed, will dictate that Governments long established should not be changed for light and transient causes; and accordingly all experience hath shewn, that mankind are more disposed to suffer, while evils are sufferable, than to right themselves by abolishing the forms to which they are accustomed. But when a long train of abuses and usurpations, pursuing invariably the same Object evinces a design to reduce them under absolute Despotism, it is their right, it is their duty, to throw off such Government, and to provide new Guards for their future security. — Such has been the patient sufferance of these Colonies; and such is now the necessity which constrains them to alter their former Systems of Government. The history of the present King of Great Britain is a history of repeated injuries and usurpations, all having in direct object the establishment of an absolute Tyranny over these States. To prove this, let Facts be submitted to a candid world. — He has refused his Assent to Laws, the most wholesome and necessary for the public good. — He has forbidden his Governors to pass Laws of immediate and pressing importance, unless suspended in their operation till his Assent should be obtained; and when so suspended, he has utterly neglected to attend to them. — He has refused to pass other Laws for the accommodation of large districts of people, unless those people would relinquish the right of Representation in the Legislature, a right inestimable to them and formidable to tyrants only. — He has called together legislative bodies at places unusual, uncomfortable, and distant from the depository of their Public Records, for the sole purpose of fatiguing them into compliance with his measures. — He has dissolved Representative Houses repeatedly, for opposing with manly firmness his invasions on the rights of the people. — He has refused for a long time, after such dissolutions, to cause others to be elected; whereby the Legislative powers, incapable of Annihilation, have returned to the People at large for their exercise; the State remaining in the mean time exposed to all the dangers of invasion from without, and convulsions within. — He has endeavoured to prevent the population of these States; for that purpose obstructing the Laws for Naturalization of Foreigners; refusing to pass others to encourage their migrations hither, and raising the conditions of new Appropriations of Lands. — He has obstructed the Administration of Justice, by refusing his Assent to Laws for establishing Judiciary powers. — He has made Judges dependent on his Will alone, for the tenure of their offices, and the amount and payment of their salaries. — He has erected a multitude of New Offices, and sent hither swarms of Officers to harrass our people, and eat out their substance. — He has kept among us, in times of peace, Standing Armies without the Consent of our legislatures. — He has affected to render the Military independent of and superior to the Civil power. — He has combined with others to subject us to a jurisdiction foreign to our constitution, and unacknowledged by our laws; giving his Assent to their Acts of pretended Legislation: — For quartering large bodies of armed troops among us: — For protecting them, by a mock Trial, from punishment for any Murders which they should commit on the Inhabitants of these States: — For cutting off our Trade with all parts of the world: — For imposing Taxes on us without our Consent: — For depriving us in many cases, of the benefits of Trial by Jury: — For transporting us beyond Seas to be tried for pretended offences — For abolishing the free System of English Laws in a neighbouring Province, establishing therein an Arbitrary government, and enlarging its Boundaries so as to render it at once an example and fit instrument for introducing the same absolute rule into these Colonies: — For taking away our Charters, abolishing our most valuable Laws, and altering fundamentally the Forms of our Governments: — For suspending our own Legislatures, and declaring themselves invested with power to legislate for us in all cases whatsoever. — He has abdicated Government here, by declaring us out of his Protection and waging War against us. — He has plundered our seas, ravaged our Coasts, burnt our towns, and destroyed the lives of our people. — He is at this time transporting large Armies of foreign Mercenaries to compleat the works of death, desolation and tyranny, already begun with circumstances of Cruelty & perfidy scarcely paralleled in the most barbarous ages, and totally unworthy the Head of a civilized nation. — He has constrained our fellow Citizens taken Captive on the high Seas to bear Arms against their Country, to become the executioners of their friends and Brethren, or to fall themselves by their Hands. — He has excited domestic insurrections amongst us, and has endeavoured to bring on the inhabitants of our frontiers, the merciless Indian Savages, whose known rule of warfare, is an undistinguished destruction of all ages, sexes and conditions. In every stage of these Oppressions We have Petitioned for Redress in the most humble terms: Our repeated Petitions have been answered only by repeated injury. A Prince, whose character is thus marked by every act which may define a Tyrant, is unfit to be the ruler of a free people. Nor have We been wanting in attentions to our British brethren. We have warned them from time to time of attempts by their legislature to extend an unwarrantable jurisdiction over us. We have reminded them of the circumstances of our emigration and settlement here. We have appealed to their native justice and magnanimity, and we have conjured them by the ties of our common kindred to disavow these usurpations, which, would inevitably interrupt our connections and correspondence. They too have been deaf to the voice of justice and of consanguinity. We must, therefore, acquiesce in the necessity, which denounces our Separation, and hold them, as we hold the rest of mankind, Enemies in War, in Peace Friends. —

We, therefore, the Representatives of the united States of America, in General Congress, Assembled, appealing to the Supreme Judge of the world for the rectitude of our intentions, do, in the Name, and by Authority of the good People of these Colonies, solemnly publish and declare, That these United Colonies are, and of Right ought to be Free and Independent States; that they are Absolved from all Allegiance to the British Crown, and that all political connection between them and the State of Great Britain, is and ought to be totally dissolved; and that as Free and Independent States, they have full Power to levy War, conclude Peace, contract Alliances, establish Commerce, and to do all other Acts and Things which Independent States may of right do. — And for the support of this Declaration, with a firm reliance on the protection of divine Providence, we mutually pledge to each other our Lives, our Fortunes and our sacred Honor.

John Hancock

Button Gwinnett
Lyman Hall
Geo Walton.

Wm Hooper
Joseph Hewes,
John Penn

Edward Rutledge.

Thos Heyward Junr.
Thomas Lynch Junr.
Arthur Middleton

Samuel Chase
Wm Paca
Thos Stone
Charles Carroll of Carrollton

George Wythe
Richard Henry Lee
Th Jefferson
Benja Harrison
Thos Nelson jr.
Francis Lightfoot Lee
Carter Braxton

Robt Morris
Benjamin Rush
Benja Franklin
John Morton
Geo Clymer
Jas Smith
Geo Taylor
James Wilson
Geo Ross
Caesar Rodney
Geo Read
Tho McKean

Wm Floyd
Phil. Livingston
Frans Lewis
Lewis Morris

Richd Stockton
Jno Witherspoon
Fras Hopkinson
John Hart
Abra Clark

CHAPTER ONE

U.S. Censorship History

I N MAY 1775, REPRESENTATIVES FROM THE THIRTEEN British colonies in North America began meeting in Philadelphia, Pennsylvania. The colonists had just launched a military rebellion against Great Britain. The group meeting in Philadelphia was called the Second Continental Congress. It directed the war and made plans for the colonies to shake off British rule.

On July 4, 1776, the Congress approved the Declaration of Independence. This statement announced that the thirteen colonies were no longer a part of the British Empire. They had become independent states—the United States of America. The document also explained why Americans wanted independence. Among other things, it said:

> We hold these Truths to be self-evident, that all men are created equal, that they are endowed by their Creator with certain unalienable Rights, that among these are Life, Liberty and the Pursuit of Happiness.

Since the Declaration of Independence *(left)* in 1776, the world has seen the United States as a land of liberty. But freedom has its limits.

15

Ever since that declaration, the United States has been a symbol of freedom to many people around the world. Indeed, liberty is a key element of U.S. law and culture. But even in the United States, freedom is not absolute.

FREEDOM OF SPEECH

The U.S. Constitution, adopted in 1787, defines the basic principles and laws of the United States. It describes the three main branches of U.S. government:

the executive branch, headed by the president; the legislative branch, made up of Congress; and the judicial branch, or federal courts. It carefully outlines the powers of each branch.

The government added ten amendments, or changes, to the U.S. Constitution in 1791. These amendments, called the Bill of Rights, describe the specific rights of U.S. citizens. The Bill of Rights prevents the government from denying important individual freedoms.

Below: The Bill of Rights guarantees freedom of speech to Americans. The government has restricted that speech in certain cases.

The First Amendment defines one of the most cherished U.S. rights: freedom of speech. This amendment reads:

> Congress shall make no law respecting an establishment of religion, or prohibiting the free exercise thereof; or abridging [limiting] the freedom of speech, or of the press, or the right of the people peaceably to assemble, and to petition the Government for a redress of grievances [righting of wrongs].

This amendment guarantees Americans the right to speak, write, and publish anything they like, without fear of punishment. Over the centuries, the U.S. government has made some exceptions to this guarantee, however. Modern U.S. law allows the government to suppress specific types of undesirable speech. Such suppression is called censorship.

U.S. CENSORSHIP BASICS

Americans believe that to govern themselves well, they must be able to share ideas—even controversial ones—freely. For this reason, U.S. law generally protects speech that criticizes the government. It also protects speech supporting distasteful or unpopular ideas, such as racism.

But the law limits some kinds of speech. For example, speech that puts people in "clear and present danger" is not protected. In the United States, a person does not have the right to walk into a crowded theater and shout "Fire!" when no fire exists. This type of speech could make theatergoers panic and trample others in their haste to exit the building.

U.S. law also limits other types of speech. Among these are obscenity (speech that many people consider vulgar, raunchy, or disgusting), defamation (lying to harm others), and speech intended to provoke violence. The U.S. government does not curb such speech in a random, biased, or sweeping way. Rather, it tries to limit speech sparingly. The government also regulates different types of speech in different ways.

Americans disagree sharply on how to interpret and apply the First Amendment. But they do agree on a basic strategy. Ideally, U.S. law should not curb speech unless censorship is the best—or only—way to achieve an important public goal.

How did U.S. law arrive at its current state? And how has the developing law affected public speech—especially on the Internet? Answering these questions requires a look at the legal history of public speech in the United States.

A FREE PRESS?

Censorship existed in the United States from its beginnings. In the early United States, some towns and cities had censorship laws. And despite the First Amendment, the federal government began censoring the press in 1798. That year Congress passed the Alien and Sedition Acts. (The word *alien* refers to foreigners, and *sedition* means "stirring up rebellion against authority.") Among other things, this set of four laws banned speech that was critical of the U.S. government. By 1802 Congress had either let the laws expire or had repealed (voided) them because they were deemed to be unconstitutional.

As the 1800s wore on, the issue of slavery took center stage. In the northern states, where slavery had been outlawed, many people opposed slavery. They wanted the government to abolish, or do away with, the practice altogether. In the South, where slavery was common, some people wanted to silence the abolitionists. In some parts of the South, newspapers could not publish articles supporting abolition and the postal service refused to deliver mail to abolitionists.

The debate over slavery eventually led to the Civil War (1861–1865). This war pitted the federal government against a group of states in the South that had withdrawn from the rest of the country. During the war, President Abraham Lincoln shut down newspapers that revealed the federal government's military strategies or that sympathized with the South.

MORAL CRUSADERS

In the late 1800s, the government took aim at a different kind of speech. In this instance, censorship was an attempt to improve morality, or good behavior, in U.S. society.

Named for Anthony Comstock *(above)*, the Comstock Act of 1873 led to widespread censorship of written materials.

Anthony Comstock served as a soldier in the Civil War. After the war, Comstock moved to New York City and worked as a postal inspector. He was a devout Christian. In his view, the city was filled with sin— especially sexual wickedness. To combat this evil, Comstock founded an organization called the New York Society for the Suppression of Vice (immorality). He began a crusade to ban all written materials that he considered lewd, or indecent.

In 1873 Comstock persuaded Congress to pass the nation's first federal antiobscenity law. It was part of a larger law governing the U.S. Postal Service. The new law, commonly known as the Comstock Act, was formally named An Act for the Suppression of Trade in, and Circulation of, Obscene Literature and Articles of Immoral Use. The law banned the manufacture, purchase, sale, advertisement, loan, gift, publication,   transport, or possession of any item that mentioned or depicted sex, birth control, or abortion. Violators of the Comstock Act faced steep fines and prison time.

The Comstock ban was sweeping. It even applied to private letters, medical texts, educational materials, and literary works. Among other things, people used the law to block sex education and to censor books. Over the next century, federal lawmakers amended the Comstock Act several times. But they never repealed it.

The Comstock Act found widespread support in the city of Boston, Massachusetts—especially among the city's social and political elites. Comstock's New York Society for the Suppression of Vice inspired Bostonians to form a group of their own in 1878. This group, the Watch and Ward Society, adopted the mission to "watch and ward off evildoers" by banning books and censoring the performing arts. As a result, Boston became a U.S. censorship headquarters in the late 1800s and early 1900s.

With the Watch and Ward Society's help, city officials strangled Boston's literary and artistic community. Officials seized books and ran theatrical shows out of town. They blocked movie showings or stopped them mid-reel. Meanwhile, the Boston Public Library kept questionable books in a locked room. Publishers and booksellers withheld books from the public for fear of legal trouble. Some theaters put on censored "Boston versions" of shows.

The Watch and Ward Society successfully stamped out what it considered indecency in Boston's public life. But this movement had unintended results. Boston's stature as a cultural center suffered severely. And outside Boston, some people ridiculed the city's zealous censorship. If a work had been "banned in Boston," this meant it was sexy or raunchy—and that's exactly what many Americans wanted to buy. Some promoters falsely labeled their works "banned in Boston" to titillate, or excite, the public and increase sales.

Books Attacked by the Comstock Act

The following is a partial list of books banned under the Comstock Act of 1873. Banning meant different things for different books. For example, a banned book published abroad could not be imported into or published in a new edition within the United States. If a book was already circulating in the United States, government officials or vice societies might remove it from library or bookstore shelves. In modern times, many of the banned works are considered literary classics.

All Quiet on the Western Front by Erich Maria Remarque (Germany, 1929)

An American Tragedy by Theodore Dreiser (United States, 1925)

Candide by Voltaire (France, 1759)

The Decameron by Giovanni Boccaccio (Italy, circa 1350)

For Whom the Bell Tolls by Ernest Hemingway (United States 1940)

Gargantua and Pantagruel by Francois Rabelais (France, 1500s)

God's Little Acre by Erskine Caldwell (United States, 1933)

Lady Chatterley's Lover by D. H. Lawrence (United Kingdom, 1928)

Leaves of Grass by Walt Whitman (United States, 1855)

Point Counter Point by Aldous Huxley (United Kingdom, 1928)

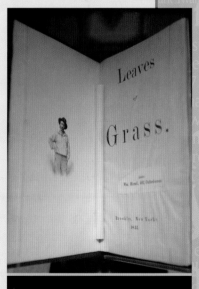

Above: Leaves of Grass by Walt Whitman was banned in Boston in the 1880s for frank poems about sexuality.

Above: In Boston the Watch and Ward Society kept a close eye on libraries and booksellers. This image shows the Boston Library in the early 1900s.

THE EARLY 1900s: POLITICAL CENSORSHIP

After the Boston antiobscenity crusade, another censorship movement began in Washington, D.C. In April 1917, the United States entered World War I (1914–1918). U.S. president Woodrow Wilson didn't want people speaking out against the war. He believed such dissent harmed the morale of soldiers and threatened the U.S. cause.

So in June 1917, Wilson urged Congress to pass the Espionage Act. The word *espionage* means "spying or passing secret information to an enemy." Most nations consider spying a serious crime. But the Espionage Act of 1917 greatly expanded the legal meaning of *espionage* in the United States. Under the act, it was a crime to express any public opinions that could help the enemy, cause disobedience within the U.S. military, or hinder military recruiting or enlistment. A person didn't have to reveal any secrets to the enemy or have any contact with the enemy to be accused of espionage.

The next year, federal law clamped down even harder on political speech. In 1918 President Wilson—still worried about dissent against the war—urged Congress to strengthen the Espionage Act.

Lawmakers responded by passing a new version of the law, called the Sedition Act. The Sedition Act of 1918 forbade spoken or printed criticism of the U.S. government, constitution, or flag. The act also allowed the U.S. Postal Service to deny mail delivery to people who disagreed with government policy during wartime.

Above: President Woodrow Wilson used the Espionage Act of 1917 to quiet dissent in the United States during World War I.

Some Americans challenged the Sedition Act in court. In 1919 three different cases reached the U.S. Supreme Court, the nation's highest court. In all three cases, the Court supported the censorship law. In *Schenck v. United States*, for instance, the Court upheld the conviction of a man who had published leaflets urging Americans to resist the draft (mandatory military service). Explaining the Court's decision, Justice Oliver Wendell Holmes Jr. wrote:

> The question in every case is whether the words used are used in such circumstances and are of such a nature as to create a clear and present danger.... When a nation is at war, many things that might be said in time of peace are such a hindrance to its effort that their utterance will not be endured.

The court reached similar conclusions in the other cases, *Debs v. United States* and *Abrams v. United States*. These cases concerned antiwar speeches and publications. In the latter case, however, Holmes disagreed with the majority of justices. He appeared to have had a change of heart. In his dissenting opinion, Holmes wrote, "The ultimate good desired is better reached by free trade in ideas ... the best test of truth is the power of the thought to get itself accepted in the competition of the market." In other words, Holmes believed, people would accept good ideas and reject bad ones, and the distinction would be made only by letting people hear these ideas to decide for themselves.

> **When a nation is at war, many things that might be said in time of peace are such a hindrance to its effort that their utterance will not be endured.**
>
> —SUPREME COURT JUSTICE OLIVER WENDELL HOLMES JR., 1919

> **"The ultimate good desired is better reached by free trade in ideas . . . the best test of truth is the power of the thought to get itself accepted in the competition of the market."**
>
> **—SUPREME COURT JUSTICE OLIVER WENDELL HOLMES JR.,** 1919

In writing these two opinions, Holmes illustrated the tension between free speech and censorship in the United States. The ideas work side by side in U.S. society, and both aim to protect the public. Holmes, like most Americans, struggled over the best way to balance them.

Above: Justice Oliver Wendell Holmes Jr. wrote key arguments during the Supreme Court censorship cases of 1919.

CHALLENGING CENSORSHIP

During and just after World War I, officials arrested and imprisoned hundreds of antiwar activists under the Espionage Act and the Sedition Act. Concerned citizens formed the National Civil Liberties Bureau (NCLB) to provide legal aid to people arrested under the acts.

The NCLB changed its name to the American Civil Liberties Union (ACLU) in 1920. The ACLU pledged to work in U.S. courts, legislatures, and communities to preserve the individual rights guaranteed by U.S. law. The ACLU became a protector of freedom of speech and strongly influenced the development of constitutional law.

Above: During World War I, the government used the Espionage Act and the Sedition Act to silence dissenters, such as these U.S. antiwar activists in Washington, D.C.

Congress repealed the Espionage Act and the Sedition Act in 1921. Large parts of the Espionage Act remained part of U.S. law, however. These remnants allow the government to classify information (hide it from the general public) for national security reasons.

In 1925 the Supreme Court heard *Gitlow v. New York*, another important case concerning freedom of speech. The Court resolved a long-standing debate by ruling that the First Amendment applies not only to the federal government but also to the states. The Court based its ruling on the Fourteenth Amendment, which was adopted in 1868. This amendment reads, in part:

> No State shall make or enforce any law which shall abridge [limit] the privileges or immunities [protections] of citizens of the United States; nor shall any State deprive any person of life, liberty, or property, without due process of law; nor deny to any person within its jurisdiction equal protection of the laws.

The First Amendment refers specifically to Congress and the federal government. *Gitlow v. New York* established that the Fourteenth Amendment makes the First Amendment applicable to the states as well.

CENSORSHIP AT MID-CENTURY

In the 1930s, legal developments regarding freedom of speech continued to focus on national security and morality. In 1931 the Supreme Court recognized that the First Amendment can protect nonverbal "speech." The case involved Yetta Stromberg, a member of the Young Communist League. Communists desire a political system in which the government controls the economy, with no private business or private property. Stromberg had displayed a red flag, a Communist emblem, as a protest against the U.S. government. A California court had convicted Stromberg of a felony for this act. But the Supreme

Yetta Stromberg *(above)* promoted Communism, a political system that appalled many Americans. In 1931 the Supreme Court upheld her right to freely express her views.

Court reversed this conviction. It found that the California law had improperly restricted Stromberg's First Amendment right to free expression.

The same year, a separate Supreme Court decision set an important precedent (legal model) on the issue of freedom of the press. The *Saturday Press* was a small newspaper in Minneapolis, Minnesota. It published sensational (dramatic and lurid) reports of city officials' illegal activities. The newspaper's owner was Jay Near. Near's critics called his paper a scandal sheet. They said he used his newspaper to harass people, especially Catholics, Jews, African Americans, and members of labor unions. A local court silenced the paper based on the Minnesota Gag Law of 1925. This law allowed the state government to shut down "a malicious, scandalous and defamatory newspaper, magazine or other periodical."

Near appealed to the Minnesota Supreme Court, which upheld the local court's decision. Then he took his case to the U.S. Supreme Court. The high court overturned the lower court decisions. It found the Minnesota Gag Law to be unconstitutional because it violated the right to press freedom. Explaining the high court's decision, Chief Justice Charles Hughes quoted British judge and historian William Blackstone: "The liberty of the press is indeed essential to the nature of a free state ... this [liberty] consists in laying no previous restraints upon publications."

Near v. Minnesota established a principle that has stood firm ever since. U.S. law considers censorship of the press unacceptable except in rare cases, such as those concerning national security. This principle has prevented politicians from censoring journalists. As a result, the press acts as a public watchdog—exposing wrongdoing on the part of politicians, businesspeople, and others.

Later in the 1930s, a different sort of speech struggle took place. With help from Morris Ernst, a lawyer and ACLU founder, publishers waged two successful fights against censorship of so-called obscenity.

Irish author James Joyce had written an epic novel titled *Ulysses.* A U.S. literary journal had partially published the book in installments from 1918 to 1920. One chapter included an overtly sexual scene. After the chapter's publication, the New York Society for the Suppression of Vice had spoken out against the novel. In 1921 the courts had declared *Ulysses* obscene and banned its publication in the United States.

More than a decade later, a U.S. publisher imported a French edition of the book. Officials seized the shipment, and the publisher hired Ernst to challenge the seizure in court. In 1933 a federal judge ruled that *Ulysses* was a serious work of literary art. He said that its potentially offensive elements were

The novel *Ulysses* by James Joyce *(above)* was initially banned in the United States because of sexual content.

honest expressions of Joyce's fictional characters. Thus the book was neither obscene nor illegal in the United States. This decision allowed Americans to import and publish other serious literature that contained coarse language or sexual subject matter.

In 1938 another periodical fought a different kind of obscenity charge. The April 1938 issue of *Life* magazine contained a feature titled "Birth of a Baby." The article explained the stages of human pregnancy and birth using diagrams, photos, and text. It showed no nudity or sexual acts.

As soon as the issue hit newsstands, police and vice societies across the United States conducted raids. They seized the magazines and arrested vendors. A prosecuting attorney charged that the photographs and drawings were "disgusting, obscene, indecent and unlawful" and "would suggest impure and libidinous [lustful] thoughts in the young and inexperienced."

Life countered that "Birth of a Baby" was actually good for youths. Rather than encourage sexual activity, the article would correct misconceptions about sex, the magazine argued. Ernst called the ban "an attack on public health and welfare" and argued, "*Life* is not obscene unless human birth is." A New York court ruled in *Life*'s favor. This decision opened the door to publications on reproductive issues. It was an important step forward in health education.

Above: Life magazine publisher Roy Larsen *(right)* sells a copy of the 1938 "Birth of a Baby" issue to police detective Frank C. McCarthy to deliberately challenge censorship laws.

After World War II (1939–1945) broke out in Europe, U.S. lawmakers were worried about revolution (overthrow of the government) in the United States. They especially worried about Communists, whose leaders had staged a revolution in the Soviet Union (based in modern-day Russia) several decades earlier. In 1940 Congress passed the Smith Act. This law made it illegal to advocate overthrowing the U.S. government by force or violence.

The law became famous for its use against people who wanted to see changes in U.S. society and government. In the 1940s and 1950s, the government arrested and jailed hundreds of people under the Smith Act. Many of these people had not advocated violent overthrow of the government. They simply disagreed with the U.S. form of government or promoted change of some sort.

The Supreme Court eventually threw out many Smith Act convictions as unconstitutional because they violated free-speech protections. However, the law remains on the books in revised form. In modern times, promoting peaceful change—even drastic change—in U.S. society, economics, or politics is legal. But conspiring (joining others in a plot) to urge, teach, or commit violent overthrow of the government is illegal.

In 1941 a man named Walter Chaplinsky was preaching on the sidewalks of Rochester, New Hampshire. A crowd gathered, and commotion ensued. When police officers intervened, Chaplinsky shouted and cursed at them. Police then arrested and convicted him under a state law prohibiting offensive speech directed at others in a public place. Chaplinsky appealed, and his case went to the U.S. Supreme Court.

In the 1942 case *Chaplinsky v. New Hampshire*, the high court ruled against Chaplinsky. It determined that the First Amendment does not protect "'fighting' words—those which, by their very utterance, inflict injury or tend to incite an immediate breach of the peace." Explaining the high court's decision, Justice Frank Murphy opined (argued) that "such utterances are no essential part of any exposition of ideas, and are of such slight social value as a step to truth that any benefit that may be derived from them is clearly out-weighed by the social interest in order and morality." This opinion became known as the fighting words doctrine.

> **" It has been well observed that [fighting words] are no essential part of any exposition of ideas, and are of such slight social value as a step to truth that any benefit that may be derived from them is clearly outweighed by the social interest in order and morality. "**
>
> **—SUPREME COURT JUSTICE FRANK MURPHY,** 1942

In the years since 1942, U.S. courts have reaffirmed the fighting words doctrine several times. But the Supreme Court has reversed some convictions made under this doctrine. In addition, the scope of the doctrine has steadily shrunk. Modern courts tend to define the term *fighting words* narrowly. They emphasize that fighting words must present an actual threat of immediate violence, not just offensive content. Otherwise, they are protected as free speech under the Constitution.

In the late 1940s, television was newly arrived on the media scene. Radio was only several decades old at this time. The Federal Communications Commission (FCC), the agency that regulates communications technology in the United States, decided in 1949 that both radio and television should present controversial issues in a balanced way—with equal time given to views on all sides of the issue.

> " A function of free speech . . . is to invite dispute. It may indeed best serve its high purpose when it induces a condition of unrest, creates dissatisfaction with conditions as they are, or even stirs people to anger. "
>
> —SUPREME COURT JUSTICE WILLIAM O. DOUGLAS, 1949

This policy was called the fairness doctrine. Many broadcasters and journalists opposed the doctrine. They believed it violated their freedom of speech. But the law remained in place.

CHANGING CULTURE, CHANGING LAWS

From the 1950s through the 1970s, public debate over free speech focused heavily on moral issues. On one side of the debate, those with traditional views sought to protect society—especially youth—from moral corruption. On the other side of the debate, various organizations and individuals worked to uphold constitutional protection of free speech.

In 1952 the Supreme Court found for the first time that free speech protections apply to motion pictures. Prior to this case, *Joseph Burstyn, Inc. v. Wilson*, movie studios had to comply with a strict censorship code. They could not include sexually suggestive dialogue or scenes in films. In *Burstyn v. Wilson*, the Court ruled that cinema was an art form worthy of First Amendment protection. This decision started a steady decline in motion picture censorship in the United States.

An important obscenity case took place in 1957. A Michigan law said that any printed matter with obscene language was illegal because it could corrupt children. In *Butler v. Michigan*, the Supreme Court struck down this law. Explaining the court's decision, Justice Felix Frankfurter wrote: The law "reduce[s] the adult population of Michigan to reading only what is fit for children." He also explained that the law trampled personal freedoms necessary "for the maintenance and progress of a free society."

A decade later, the high court ruled on the obscenity issue again in *Ginsberg v. New York*. Sam Ginsberg ran a small store and lunch counter in Bellmore, New York. On two occasions in October 1965, Ginsberg sold a "girlie" magazine to a sixteen-year-old boy. Ginsberg was arrested for and convicted of breaking a state law that forbade selling any material that showed nudity or sexual conduct to a minor.

In his 1968 appeal to the Supreme Court, Ginsberg argued that the New York law violated the boy's right to read under the First Amendment. The Court disagreed. It found that the law did not violate the child's rights because the material in question was obscene—and therefore harmful to children. The Court's ruling thus set stricter obscenity standards for children than for adults.

The next year further clarified the relationship between obscenity and children in the eyes of the law. In 1969 the Supreme Court decision *Stanley v. Georgia* ruled that while states could regulate the distribution of obscene material to protect youth, states could not punish private possession of obscene material. This case established a personal right to privacy in U.S. law.

In 1973 the Supreme Court decision *Miller v. California* established a much-needed test for determining whether public speech was obscene and therefore not protected by the First Amendment. This test has remained in place ever since. Chief Justice Warren Burger outlined the definition of obscenity:

> The basic guidelines ... must be: (a) whether "the average person, applying contemporary community standards" would find that the work, taken as a whole, appeals to the

prurient [sexual] interest; (b) whether the work depicts or describes, in a patently offensive way, sexual conduct specifically defined by the applicable state law; and (c) whether the work, taken as a whole, lacks serious literary, artistic, political, or scientific value.

Miller v. California was a landmark case because it defined obscenity. It gave states greater power to censor obscene material. In fact, hundreds of obscenity trials went forward around the nation immediately after this ruling.

THE MARKETPLACE OF IDEAS

Before and during World War II, the National Socialist Party, or Nazis, ruled Germany. The Nazis carried out the imprisonment and organized slaughter of millions of European Jews and other minority peoples. This slaughter is called the Holocaust.

In 1976 the National Socialist Party of America (NSPA) planned a march in the Chicago suburb of Skokie, Illinois. Skokie was a mainly Jewish community and was home to many Holocaust survivors.

At their protests, NSPA members typically wore and displayed the swastika, a symbol of Nazi Germany. Skokie residents argued that for Holocaust survivors, seeing the swastika brought back horrific memories. It was just like being physically attacked. The Village of Skokie denied the NSPA a permit for public demonstration.

The NSPA pursued its case in Illinois courts and the U.S. Supreme Court. After several appeals in 1977 and 1978, the courts allowed the NSPA to march. They ruled that the swastika is symbolic speech deserving of First Amendment protection. The courts also determined that the swastika did not constitute fighting words.

The Skokie case showed that the First Amendment protects not only views that most people support but also unpopular beliefs. The First Amendment makes possible the marketplace of ideas that Oliver Wendell Holmes described in 1919. This marketplace promotes the

Above: In court decisions in the 1970s, the right of Nazi groups to speak freely in the United States was upheld. The First Amendment protects even unpopular or offensive speech.

greater good by welcoming all views, encouraging debate, and permitting the best ideas to win support on their strength alone.

In 1982 the Supreme Court made an important ruling on pornography—words or images that depict sexual behavior. In *New York v. Ferber*, the Court decided that the government could ban child pornography (images of minors or people who appear to be minors engaging in sexual activities) without first using the *Miller v. California* guidelines to determine whether the material was obscene. The justices reasoned that making child pornography is inherently and gravely harmful to children and that the government has a strong interest in protecting children from such harm. The justices determined that to effectively protect children from the making of child pornography, the government also needed to ban its advertisement, sale, and distribution. Eight years later, the high court extended this ban to the mere possession of child pornography.

Freedom to parody is upheld

From the Pages of
USA TODAY

Hustler magazine publisher Larry Flynt is the winner over Rev. Jerry Falwell in a legal battle that has press groups and cartoonists cheering from the sidelines.

The Supreme Court's unanimous ruling Wednesday says public figures like Falwell cannot recover money damages for "emotional distress" they suffer from satires such as the bawdy ad parody in a 1984 *Hustler.* A jury had awarded Falwell $200,000.

Written by Chief Justice William Rehnquist—not usually a press ally—the decision was applauded by media advocates who had feared a new wave of lawsuits against artists and writers who use satire.

Above: Larry Flynt holds up a copy of the controversial parody of the Reverend Jerry Falwell that appeared in Flynt's pornographic magazine *Hustler* in 1984.

Jerry Falwell *(center)*, with his wife and lawyer, speaks to reporters during the 1987 Supreme Court case.

"I've always considered Flynt a slimeball, but he isn't the only winner," said sharp-penned Pulitzer Prize-winning cartoonist Mike Peters of the Dayton (Ohio) *Daily News*. "The Mark Twains, the James Thurbers, the H.L. Menckens, every artist and satirist is a winner" Reaction:

- "No sleaze merchant like Larry Flynt should be able to use the First Amendment as an excuse for maliciously and dishonestly attacking public figures," said Falwell.
- "I spent over $1 million in attorney's fees," said Flynt. "It's what you call paying to defend the First Amendment."
- "A resounding victory for the idea that the First Amendment protects speech that makes us uncomfortable," said Bruce Sanford of the Society of Professional Journalists.
- "It's distressing for those who feel the press already goes far enough," said Michael McDonald of the conservative Washington Legal Foundation.

—Tony Mauro

www.usatoday.com

News
SECTION A

June 22, 1987

Fairness doctrine vetoed

From the Pages of
USA TODAY

The fairness doctrine—the 38-year-old government policy that requires broadcasters to give both sides of controversial issues—died over the weekend at the hands of a presidential veto. "In any other medium besides broadcasting, such federal policing of the editorial judgment of journalists would be unthinkable," President [Ronald] Reagan said. The "Fairness in Broadcasting Act of 1987," which passed the House 302–102 and the Senate 59–31, resulted from a push by the FCC to dump the policy and give broadcasters the same First Amendment rights as newspapers.... The House passed the law with the two-thirds majority needed to override a veto; the Senate did not.

—Adell Crowe

Meanwhile, the fairness doctrine continued to cause controversy. Many people wanted the policy revoked as a violation of freedom of speech. In 1987 the Supreme Court ruled the fairness doctrine to be constitutional, but the Court also found that because the policy wasn't a federal law, it needn't be enforced. Members of Congress who supported the fairness doctrine then passed a bill that did make the doctrine into federal law. But President Ronald Reagan vetoed (rejected) the bill. This act simultaneously killed the old fairness doctrine and the new law.

The following year, free speech advocates won another victory with the help of an unlikely hero, Larry Flynt. Flynt published *Hustler*, a magazine known for its crude humor and explicit pictures of nude women. In 1983 *Hustler* had published a fake advertisement ridiculing Jerry Falwell, a prominent Christian minister. The sexually explicit ad mocked not only Falwell but also his mother.

Falwell sued Flynt for intentionally causing him emotional distress. A U.S. district court ruled in Falwell's favor and awarded him two hundred thousand dollars in damages, or compensation for the harm he had endured. Flynt challenged the decision in a U.S. circuit court and lost. Then he took his appeal to the Supreme Court. The high court favored Flynt. It ruled in *Hustler Magazine Inc. v. Falwell* that "to protect the free flow of ideas and opinions on matters of public interest and concern, the First and Fourteenth Amendments prohibit public figures and public officials from recovering damages for . . . intentional infliction of emotional distress."

CHAPTER TWO

Censorship in the Internet Age

THE 1980s BROUGHT THE WORLD A NEW AND revolutionary form of communication. Since the 1960s, the U.S. government had been slowly linking its local computer networks with one another, as well as with university networks. In 1982 computer engineers agreed upon standard methods for transmitting data among networks. This standardization sped up the linking of networks around the world. Soon a global network of networks existed. This meganetwork became known as the Internet.

In the late 1980s, the Internet opened up to business use. Commercial Internet service providers (ISPs) and e-mail services entered the scene. And in 1989, the World Wide Web was born. The World Wide Web is a system of linked documents, or Web pages, stored on the Internet.

In the early 1990s, engineers developed easy-to-use Web browsers—tools that help users navigate among the many Web pages on the Internet. Web browsers

Left: Internet communication has exploded since the late 1980s, creating a host of challenges for citizens and lawmakers.

caused an explosion in Web use in the mid-1990s. In the twenty-first century, the Internet carries a vast array of online services. These include e-mail, online chat, file sharing, gaming, social networking, online broadcasting, video on demand, and interpersonal voice and video communication.

The Internet lets people share huge amounts of information with one another quickly and easily. It's a communication tool unlike any other. Its power to distribute knowledge and connect people offers great promise to humankind. So what's the problem? For one thing, the Internet makes it possible to spread inaccurate, offensive, dangerous, private, illegal, and otherwise inappropriate information easily too. One example is pornography, including child pornography, which exploded with the Internet revolution.

ELECTRIFYING THE FIRST AMENDMENT

When the United States formed, the printing press was the world's primary communication technology. And the nation's founders recognized that press freedom was key to democracy. Through the First Amendment, they gave the press protection from government control.

In the late nineteenth and early twentieth centuries, new communication technologies—telephones, movies, radio, and television—appeared. Policy makers were slow to give new media the freedoms of the press, even though they performed some of the same functions as the press.

As each new medium developed, judges, lawyers, businesspeople, and scholars methodically assessed whether it deserved constitutional protection. "The moving picture screen, the radio, the newspaper, the handbill . . . and the street corner orator have differing natures, values, abuses and dangers. Each . . . is a law unto itself," explained Supreme Court justice Robert Jackson in 1949. Justice Byron White pointed out in 1969 that the "differences in the characteristics of new media justify differences in the First Amendment standards applied to them."

The Maryland State Board of Censors *(above)* meets to review movies in 1970. In the Internet age, it's much harder for regulators to review and restrict pornographic materials.

The newest media of all, the Internet, is complex and ever changing. It combines many of the functions of telephones, film, television, radio, and print media and performs other functions as well. Its capabilities change almost daily. So the courts have had to move quickly to get a handle on censorship and freedom of speech in the Internet age.

CPPA AND CDA

The first major U.S. Internet censorship battle broke out over sexually explicit content. The United States already had laws prohibiting child pornography and restricting obscenity. But many Americans worried that such content was very easy to distribute—and too easy for children to find—online. They feared that without strict regulation, the Internet might do children great harm.

In 1996 Congress passed two laws meant to address this concern. The first was the Child Pornography Prevention Act (CPPA). The CPPA extended existing federal laws against distributing and possessing child pornography to include child pornography created or distributed via computer. The law also expanded the definition of child pornography to include computer-generated images.

Six years later, the Supreme Court struck down the CPPA. The Court found that banning sexual images showing "virtual" children—that is, where no real children were involved—violated the First Amendment. However, the CPPA's spirit lives on in a law passed immediately after its demise: the Prosecutorial Remedies and Other Tools to end the Exploitation of Children Today Act (Protect Act). This law contains the same prohibitions as the CPPA had but is more carefully worded to avoid violating the First Amendment.

The Communications Decency Act (CDA), also passed in 1996, was much broader (more general) than the CPPA. It criminalized using the Internet knowingly to send or display "in a manner available to a person under 18 years of age, any comment, request, suggestion, proposal, image, or other communication that, in context, depicts or describes, in terms patently offensive as measured by contemporary community standards, sexual . . . activities or organs." Violators faced fines and up to two years in prison.

Immediately after President Bill Clinton signed the CDA into law in February 1996, opponents challenged it. A coalition of libraries, civil liberties groups, ISPs, publishers, recording companies, and individuals filed a lawsuit in federal court. They requested an injunction against the CDA (an order stopping its enforcement).

Opponents claimed that the CDA outlawed speech protected by the First Amendment. It forbade materials that were legal when published in other media, such as newspapers, magazines, or books. For example, the CDA would have criminalized the publication of classic literature such as William Shakespeare's comedies or the discussion of a wide range of sexual health topics online.

In June 1996, a panel of federal judges in Philadelphia granted the injunction. They ruled that enforcing the CDA would unconstitutionally restrict speech on the Internet. The next month, a different panel of federal judges in New York declared the CDA unconstitutional.

The federal government appealed both decisions to the U.S. Supreme Court. In June 1997, the high court upheld both lower court decisions. All nine justices voted to strike down the CDA. They found it too vague and too broad. They ruled that parental filtering software could block children's access to potentially harmful content without trampling the rights of adults. (Parents can install this software on computers to block selected types of content, such as obscene language or images.) Explaining the court's decision, Justice John Paul Stevens wrote:

Above: In 1997 Justice John Paul Stevens and his fellow Supreme Court justices agreed that the CDA violated the First Amendment.

> In order to deny minors access to potentially harmful speech, the CDA effectively suppresses a large amount of speech that adults have a constitutional right to receive and to address to one another. That burden on adult speech is unacceptable if less restrictive alternatives [filtering software] would be at least as effective in achieving the legitimate purpose that the statute was enacted to serve.

Law may make information illegal

From the Pages of
USA TODAY

A little-noticed provision of the telecommunications bill passed last week could make it a crime to put information on the Internet about abortions.

"It looks like if you were telling somebody how to use a morning-after pill [emergency birth control], that could be a felony," says Rep. Pat Schroeder, D-Colo.

A lawsuit seeking a temporary restraining order is to be filed in federal court today. It targets the broader First Amendment issues of the Communications Decency Act, which makes it illegal to put "indecent" material on-line where children could access it.

But one of the plaintiffs is [the family planning and women's health organization] Planned Parenthood. "The indecency act returns America to the days when medical information was censored," says the group's Roger Evans. "It's unconstitutional, unhealthy and unwise."

The telecommunications bill would extend the Comstock Act, an 1873 law that prohibits distribution of information about abortion, to interactive computer services.

"We do not need a bill written in 1873 governing the Internet. That's outrageous," says Schroeder. She plans to introduce an amendment to delete the provision when Congress returns from its break Feb. 26.

House Judiciary Committee Chairman Henry Hyde, R.-Ill., an author of the bill, has said the bill will not interfere with on-line debate about abortion. A Hyde spokesman says that the only difference from current law is that it is extended to interactive computer services.

"The language Rep. Schroeder is concerned about has been in the law for many, many years," says committee general counsel Alan Coffey. "This has never been enforced since Roe v. Wade" [the 1973 case upholding a woman's right to have an abortion].

But Schroeder, in a "Dear Colleague" letter to members of the House, says [the law] "provides for up to a $250,000 fine and/or five years in prison for using . . . computer services to provide or receive information about abortion."

Above: Representatives of the ACLU hold a press conference to discuss the case against the Communications Decency Act in February 1996.

Feminists agree. "Just as more women are going on-line, Congress is moving to criminalize women's constitutional right to send and receive vital medical information," says Eleanor Smeal of the Feminist Majority Foundation. Its Web site distributes information on birth control and abortions.

Among other plaintiffs in the American Civil Liberties Union suit: journalist Brock Meeks, who writes a column distributed free on the Net; the Electronic Privacy Information Center; Human Rights Watch; and Critical Path AIDS Project.

—Leslie Miller and Mike Snider

> " **As the most participatory form of mass speech yet developed, the Internet deserves the highest protection from governmental intrusion.** "
>
> —**U.S. DISTRICT COURT JUDGE STEWART DALZELL,**
> RULING ON THE CDA, 1996

COPA AND DMCA

U.S. lawmakers responded to the CDA's failure by proposing a new law right away. In October 1998, Congress passed the Child Online Protection Act (COPA). COPA was similar to the CDA but slightly more specific. COPA made it a crime to use the Web for commercial communication "harmful to minors" without restricting minors' access by requiring a credit card number. Violators faced fines of up to fifty thousand dollars and imprisonment of up to six months per violation.

Like the CDA, COPA faced immediate legal challenges. At the request of the law's opponents, a federal court promptly granted an injunction. It also found COPA unconstitutional for all the same reasons CDA was.

But unlike the CDA fight, the COPA court battle dragged on and on. The case traveled back and forth between lower courts and the Supreme Court several times. After more than a decade of appeals and review, the high court issued its final word on COPA's demise by refusing to hear any more appeals.

In the same month Congress passed COPA, it also passed another law restricting online content. The Digital Millennium Copyright Act (DMCA) was designed to prevent the copying of electronic works (text, images, audio or video files, or software) without permission from copyright owners. The DMCA makes it a crime to bypass electronic locks, or anti-copying technology, built into such works.

Napster founder Shawn Fanning *(right, with his attorney)* was at the center of a key DMCA fight. Napster lost its court battle because the free file-sharing site enabled to share copyrighted material without permission.

The DMCA has faced vocal opposition from scientists, librarians, academics, and free-speech advocates. They say it invades privacy and chills free expression, scientific research, and competition. But more than ten years later, U.S. courts have not yet ruled the law unconstitutional.

A NEW CENTURY

The new century arrived with the CDA dead and COPA dying. U.S. lawmakers had thus far failed in their efforts to prevent people from distributing indecent material online. So instead, they tried to prevent people from viewing such material.

Nashoba Regional High School
Media Center

Congress passed the Children's Internet Protection Act (CIPA) in late 2000, and it took effect in early 2001. CIPA requires schools and libraries to use Internet filters on their computers to protect children from harmful content. Schools and libraries may decline to filter Internet access. But doing so disqualifies them from receiving federal funding.

CIPA withstood a constitutional challenge in the Supreme Court two years after its enactment. The justices found that CIPA does not violate the First Amendment. They explained that Americans have no constitutional right of access to libraries and that adult library patrons can request unblocking under CIPA.

In late 2001, efforts to regulate the Internet turned sharply toward national security issues. On September 11, nineteen terrorists hijacked four U.S.

Below: CIPA requires libraries to block access to pornography and other content that might harm young Internet users.

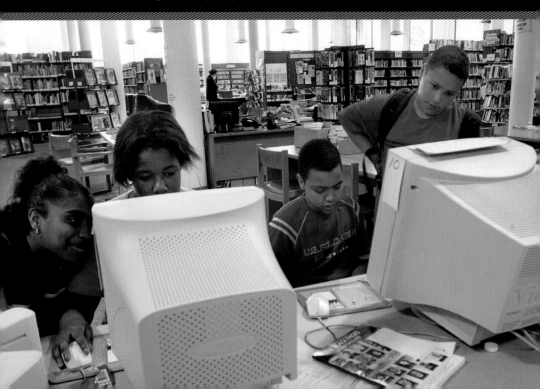

After terrorists attacked the Pentagon *(above)* in Washington, D.C., and the World Trade Center in New York on September 11, 2001, Americans called for stricter laws to regulate communications among suspected terrorists.

airliners. The terrorists intentionally crashed these planes into the twin towers of New York City's World Trade Center and into the Pentagon (U.S. Department of Defense headquarters near Washington, D.C.). The fourth plane crashed in rural Pennsylvania after its passengers tried to fight the hijackers. The attacks killed almost three thousand people, including all the hijackers, all the passengers, and many hundreds of people on the ground and inside the buildings.

Afterward, the U.S. government enacted two measures aimed at preventing more attacks. The first measure was the President's Surveillance Program (PSP). The PSP allows the government to secretly monitor electronic communications originating outside the United States to or from anyone suspected of terrorist links. The second measure was the Uniting and Strengthening America by Providing Appropriate Tools Required to Intercept and Obstruct Terrorism Act (USA

Court to Congress' online nannies: You're fired, again

From the Pages of
USA TODAY

The U.S. Supreme Court has knocked back another clumsy attempt by Congress to impose censorship on the Internet. In so doing, it has sent an implicit message to all parents: When lawmakers volunteer to baby-sit your kids, check to see whether you can do a better job yourself.

Chances are good that you can.

On Tuesday, for the third time in seven years, the court turned aside legislation that claimed to protect children by imposing major criminal penalties on Web sites that carry material perfectly legal for adults to view.

Though shielding minors from pornography is a worthwhile goal, Congress' solution is the wrong way to achieve it. Not only does the law appear to violate the First Amendment's right to free speech, but it isn't even the most effective way to curb kids' access to Internet smut.

Yet that hasn't stopped overeager members of Congress and zealous social crusaders from repeatedly trying to turn Uncle Sam into the nation's nanny.

Congress first got excited about the issue in the mid-1990s, as home-computer use surged and porn peddlers discovered the Internet as a new outlet. The result was a law written so broadly, Michelangelo's *David* [a famous nude statue] would have to don a fig leaf to avoid being prosecuted if he ventured into cyberspace.

In 1997, the Supreme Court unanimously knocked down that law as a violation of the First Amendment. Congress came back with a new version, the Child Online Protection Act signed by President Clinton in 1998.

PATRIOT Act). This federal law gave law enforcement agencies more power to search people's telephone, e-mail, medical, financial, and other records.

Both measures affected online speech in the United States by reducing the privacy of Internet users. And both underwent intense

It authorizes fines of up to $50,000 per day and six months' imprisonment for placing material "harmful to minors" within easy reach of children on the Internet.

On Tuesday, the Supreme Court sent that law back to lower courts a second time for more review of its constitutionality. But in a 5–4 ruling, the high court said the law likely violates the First Amendment.

And with good reason. Critics have argued plausibly that the law could criminalize legitimate health-advice and sex-education Web sites as well as those of bookstores, art galleries and news media.

Meanwhile, families have other choices: Internet filtering, parental monitoring and time-restricted access. Two of the most popular Web browsers, MSN and America Online, already offer a variety of parental options for curbing access to the Net's red-light district [indecent material]—plus periodic e-mail reports about children's surfing, e-mail and other activities. Several firms provide similar services for a fee. And commercial spyware programs can track which sites children visit.

Further, the high court noted, at least 40% of porn sites originate outside the USA, beyond the reach of even the most draconian federal law, and the remaining 60% could readily move offshore and stay in business if threatened. Net filters may not be perfect, but at least they stop material from any source, foreign or domestic.

The Supreme Court has long held that "obscenity"—anything that appeals to prurient interests without redeeming social or artistic value—is not protected by the First Amendment. But to curb free speech in the name of protecting children, the court says a law must be narrowly targeted and impose the least-possible restriction on the rights of adults. The version rejected Tuesday meets neither of those standards.

Whether in a family room or cyberspace, monitoring kids' behavior is best left to parents, not politicians.

—*USA TODAY* editors

congressional and judicial review in the following years. Many Americans questioned whether the laws violated the First Amendment. But both measures remained largely unchanged a decade later.

In 2003 Congress attempted to rein in e-mail spam. Spam is unsolicited mass e-mail

www.usatoday.com

News
SECTION A

June 30, 2004

Kids need law's protection

From the Pages of
USA TODAY
The Child Online Protection Act (COPA) does not censor speech. It merely requires pornographers to screen out minors by requiring identification or credit cards for adult users.

If it is OK to check the IDs of patrons at sexually oriented businesses and prohibit the selling of porn to minors, why shouldn't the same rules apply online?

The five-justice Supreme Court majority held that it may be just as effective to leave it to parents to use filters on their computers. But in the real world, filters are only partially effective and are of no use, as pornographers find ways to get around them.

The dissenting justices correctly identified the core of the problem: The pornography COPA covers is simply not entitled to constitutional protection as free speech. COPA applies to material that is either legally obscene for adults or harmful to minors.

As Justice Antonin Scalia wrote, "this business could, consistent with the First Amendment, be banned entirely, (and therefore) COPA's lesser restrictions raise no constitutional concern."

Justice Stephen Breyer added that he "cannot accept the conclusion that Congress could have accomplished its statutory [legal] objective—protecting children from commercial pornography on the Internet—in other, less-restrictive ways."

advertising. According to industry analysts, spam makes up anywhere from 75 to 97 percent of all e-mail. Although spam originates with human spammers, networks of virus-infected computers (botnets) do most of the actual distribution of e-mail spam. A lot of spam spreads viruses to recipients' computers.

Spammers say that their e-mail is the electronic equivalent of advertising sent by the U.S. Postal Service—and is therefore protected by the

> ❝ **The . . . Supreme Court . . . held that it may be just as effective to leave it to parents to use filters on their computers. But in the real world, filters are only partially effective and are of no use, as pornographers find ways to get around them.** ❞
>
> **—JAY SEKULOW** OF THE AMERICAN CENTER FOR LAW AND JUSTICE, IN SUPPORT OF COPA
>
> **✻ USA TODAY · JUNE 30, 2004**

The decision in this case, *Ashcroft vs. ACLU*, is not the end. The court ruled only that the COPA statute could not be enforced while the challenge to COPA goes to trial.

The government can still win if it can prove that COPA is the "least-restrictive means" of protecting minors from harmful material. But it will be an uphill battle.

Congress has repeatedly tried to address what everyone acknowledges is the serious problem of online porn available to kids. Each time, the Supreme Court has found fault with those efforts.

—Jay Sekulow

First Amendment. Opponents say spam is a costly nuisance. Computer users must monitor their e-mail for spam, must search for legitimate e-mail that accidentally gets caught in spam filters, and may spend hours each week deleting spam. Some companies hire staff people just to manage spam. Some spam contains pornographic images and content that many recipients find offensive. In addition, the viruses often delivered by spam can damage computers. In the end, spam costs individuals and organizations billions of dollars each year in lost human productivity, damage to computers, and other expenses.

The CAN-SPAM (Controlling the Assault of Non-Solicited Pornography and Marketing) Act of 2003 set e-mail advertising regulations. CAN-SPAM requires spammers to offer recipients an opportunity to opt out, or reject future e-mails. It also bans false headers and subject lines that might trick people into opening spam, and it establishes penalties for violators.

The CAN-SPAM Act has had little impact, however. Many spammers are experts in computer security. They easily find

Above: Senator Charles Schumer of New York displays his spam e-mail during a 2003 press conference about antispam legislation.

USA TODAY Snapshots®

Selling by spamming

More than half of all Internet e-mail is now identified as spam. Top categories:

Category	Percentage
Products	21%
Adult (porn, personal ads)	18%
Financial (investment, loan offers)	18%
Scams (chain letters, pyramid schemes)	9%
Health	6%
Leisure	6%

Source: Brightmail Logistics and Operations Center

By Joseph Popiolkowski and Sam Ward, USA TODAY, 2004

ways to avoid detection while they break the law. In fact, the cost of e-mail spam has grown each year since CAN-SPAM's passage.

As the first decade of the 2000s came to a close, lawmakers were considering more new laws regulating Internet content, access, and privacy. These proposals, like earlier ones, focused on child safety, public morality, security, and copyright issues. As the public wrestled with their implications, the Internet censorship debate raged on.

CHAPTER THREE

Child Safety

FIFTEEN-YEAR-OLD AMY MET BILL THROUGH AN INTERnet chat room. Bill, an adult, went out of his way to get to know Amy. Amy told him her dreams and desires, as well as her concerns and fears. She told Bill she wanted to live a different life. Bill sympathized with her. By showing interest and kindness toward Amy, Bill earned her trust.

One evening Amy didn't come home at her usual time. Her worried mom, Sara, searched Amy's bedroom. Sara found a note Amy had written about taking a bus trip. She also unearthed Bill's full name and address.

Meanwhile, Amy had arrived at the local bus station. She talked with Bill on the pay phone there. Bill urged her to go through with her plan to visit the town where he lived. Amy boarded the bus.

Left: The Internet gives kids access to information and entertainment. But some content can harm or endanger young users.

By the time Sara reached the bus station, Amy was gone. Sara hurried to the police station. She told the officers what had happened and gave them Bill's name and address. She begged them to intercept Amy at her destination.

The police considered Amy a runaway. Under state law, the officers said, they couldn't force a runaway to return home.

Desperate, Sara called the National Center for Missing and Exploited Children (NCMEC). The NCMEC persuaded police officers to check on Bill's name and address. They learned that Bill was a real person, and he did live at the address Sara had provided. Officers told Sara they'd watch the location.

Amy and Bill finally arrived at Bill's home in a taxi. The police couldn't legally detain either of them on the spot, but officers did convince Amy to talk to her mother by phone. Amy agreed to return home only after Sara promised not to press charges against Bill.

On the long ride home, Amy was livid. She wanted very much to be with Bill. He'd told Amy that he was in love with her. He'd promised her a happy life with him.

As mother and daughter talked, they learned a lot from each other. Amy calmed down. Sara thought the ordeal was over.

It wasn't. Amy secretly kept in touch with Bill. Three weeks later, he came to Sara and Amy's home. Amy sneaked out with him to a local motel.

Sara alerted the police, who intercepted Amy and Bill at the bus station. As the police approached, Bill told Amy that she wasn't the first girl he'd met online and lured into a face-to-face meeting. This news snapped Amy out of her fantasy. Later, she told her mom, "I can't believe I got suckered into this."

Bill was arrested, tried in court, and sentenced to one year in prison. After that he spent three years on probation (under supervision by a court official). But during his probation, Bill was arrested and tried for kidnapping another fifteen-year-old girl he'd met on the Internet. This time he received a ten-year prison sentence.

WHY ARE KIDS AT RISK ONLINE?

Amy's story illustrates one important aspect of the debate over Internet censorship: child safety. Some Americans want tighter public control over the Internet to keep children safe from predators such as Bill and from other online dangers. Other Americans insist that a combination of education and parental involvement is the best way to keep children safe online.

In the United States, a large number of children use the Internet alongside adults. And Internet usage increases with age. According to Nielsen, a company that measures digital media usage, roughly 25 percent of Americans two to eleven years old use the Internet. And 93 percent of U.S. teens twelve to seventeen years old spend time online, according to the Pew Research Center.

Experts say that these young Internet users are more susceptible to online harm than adults are. By virtue of their youth, young people have less general knowledge, less social experience, and less emotional maturity than adults have. Children are naturally trusting and optimistic. They have a normal need for attention, appreciation, and affection. If approached by a stranger online, some kids might be too trusting. They might keep the encounter a secret, either because of shame or fear or because they don't want to be tattle-tales. In addition, young people are curious about sex and other taboo

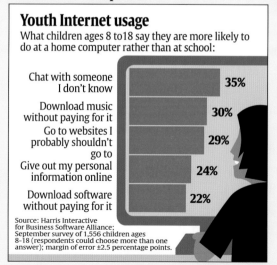

USA TODAY Snapshots®

Youth Internet usage

What children ages 8 to 18 say they are more likely to do at a home computer rather than at school:

Chat with someone I don't know	35%
Download music without paying for it	30%
Go to websites I probably shouldn't go to	29%
Give out my personal information online	24%
Download software without paying for it	22%

Source: Harris Interactive for Business Software Alliance; September survey of 1,556 children ages 8–18 (respondents could choose more than one answer); margin of error ±2.5 percentage points.

By Cindy Clark and Sam Ward, USA TODAY, 2005

Above: Most U.S. kids use the Internet regularly. Who should be responsible for limiting what they see? Parents or the government or both?

subjects. They find the Internet an easy way to explore such subjects.

In other words, children face greater risks online simply because they are children. Normal traits of children make them vulnerable to manipulation and intimidation by adults. And unfortunately, some adults don't have children's best interests at heart.

CHILDHOOD CYBERHAZARDS

What kinds of hazards do kids face online? The pitfalls are many and varied, but they all fall into two basic categories: inappropriate content and exploitation.

The Internet hosts a wealth of useful and educational information. It also hosts a lot of content that's inappropriate for children. This content includes sexually

Perils online

Survey of 1,500 kids ages 10-17:

▇ 2000 ▇ 2005

Solicitation

19%

13%

Exposure to pornography

25%

34%

Harassment

6%

9%

Source: Crimes Against Children Research Center, University of New Hampshire; margin of error ±2-3 percentage points

By Karl Gelles, USA TODAY, 2006

explicit text and photos; websites promoting hate groups or cults; sites glorifying tobacco, alcohol, and drug use; graphic violence; recipes for making explosives; and more. Depending on their maturity and the type of content, children may find such material disturbing, might believe false claims, or might develop an interest in dangerous activities.

Below: Online gambling is illegal in the United States. But many gambling websites exist anyway, and they are easily accessible to young people.

Another cyberhazard children face is exploitation. Online, children can unwittingly open the door to financial scams, hackers (people who illegally gain access to others' computers), computer viruses, or other threats. Children may become targets of cyberbullying on social networking sites or victims of electronic harassment.

Sexual predators pose the biggest exploitation risk to children. The Internet makes it easy for predators to lie about their identities, ages, and intentions. Predators frequent chat rooms looking for victims. Predators make contact with their targets and work to develop friendship, emotional connection, and interest in sexual topics. When the time seems right, a predator initiates a sexual relationship— either electronically (via pornographic photos or videos) or by meeting off-line. Predators may use money or gifts to attract

Above: Online chat is popular with kids, but sexual predators also use chat rooms to target victims.

children. They may entice children to appear in pornographic videos or photo shoots.

HOW CENSORSHIP MIGHT HELP

Some Americans believe that the best way to protect children from online dangers is to stop the dangers at their source. These people would like to see strong laws dictating the content Americans can legally post, advertise, and access on the Internet.

The United States already has laws meant to protect juvenile Internet users. For example, the Children's Online Privacy Protection Act (COPPA) took effect in 2000. COPPA requires websites to obtain parental consent before collecting or using personal information of Internet users under thirteen years old. CIPA, which took effect in 2001, requires schools and libraries to use Internet filters to protect children from harmful content such as pornography and obscenity. The Protect Act took effect in 2003. It criminalizes the creation, advertisement, or distribution of child pornography via the Internet.

Some people want more—and stronger—laws than these. Supporters say that strong laws are critical to keeping cyberspace safe for children. They are particularly concerned about the limits of filtering software. Software is not good at making human judgments about child-safe viewing: it often mistakenly permits access to inappropriate

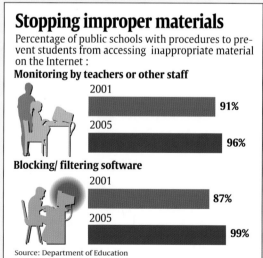

USA TODAY Snapshots®

Stopping improper materials

Percentage of public schools with procedures to prevent students from accessing inappropriate material on the Internet :

Monitoring by teachers or other staff

2001 — 91%
2005 — 96%

Blocking/ filtering software

2001 — 87%
2005 — 99%

Source: Department of Education

By David Stuckey and Robert W. Ahrens, USA TODAY, 2006

content. And many children are more computer-savvy than their parents. These children easily know their way around filtering software. Online predators and pornographers are adept at bypassing filtering software too.

Every year U.S. lawmakers propose more measures meant to restrict online content and Internet access. For example, the Deleting Online Predators Act (DOPA) of 2006 would require schools and libraries to block children's access to Internet chat rooms and social networking websites. The Keeping the Internet Devoid of Sexual Predators (KIDS) Act of 2007 would restrict Internet access for convicted sex offenders and allow authorities to monitor their computer use. The Internet Stopping Adults Facilitating the Exploitation of Today's Youth (Internet Safety) Act of 2009 would require all Internet service providers and Wi-Fi (wireless) operators to keep records about users for two years to aid police investigations. None of these proposals has yet become law. But supporters vigorously promote them.

Supporters also defend existing Internet censorship laws from First Amendment challenges. In the first decade of the 2000s, the administration of President George W. Bush was very active in fighting such challenges. For instance, in 2007, working on behalf of the federal government, U.S.

> " **Libraries have been called 'arsenals [warehouses] of liberty.' We must not allow . . . sexual predators to use our own arsenals to rob . . . our children of their innocence.** "

—FORMER U.S. REPRESENTATIVE CHIP PICKERING, SPONSOR OF CIPA

USA TODAY · MARCH 5, 2003

> **" Congress shall make no law abridging the freedom of sXXXch, or the right of the people peaceably to XXXemble, and to peXXXion the government for a redress of grievances. "**
>
> —**MARC ROTENBERG,** EXECUTIVE DIRECTOR OF THE ELECTRONIC PRIVACY INFORMATION CENTER AND PROFESSOR OF INFORMATION PRIVACY LAW AT GEORGETOWN UNIVERSITY, COMMENTING ON HOW CENSORS SOMETIMES USE XS TO MAKE WRITTEN MATERIAL ILLEGIBLE, N.D.

solicitor general Paul Clement defended the Protect Act from a First Amendment challenge in the Supreme Court. Alberto Gonzalez, a U.S. attorney general during the Bush administration, also supported strong laws to curb child pornography and clamp down on online predators. Expressing his support for the KIDS Act, Gonzalez said, "The market for sexually abusive images of children creates a dangerous environment of ever-increasing risks because children are the commodity that satisfies the insidious [treacherous], evil demands of sexual predators."

Above: Attorney General Alberto Gonzalez pushed for stronger laws to stop child pornography in the early 2000s.

PARENTING AND EDUCATION, NOT CENSORSHIP

Americans generally agree that children need protection from online dangers. But not all agree that censorship laws are the best tools to achieve this

Online predators less prevalent; Kids not as likely to be solicited, but porn, bullying increasing

From the Pages of
USA TODAY

Despite the rise of social networking sites such as MySpace, a smaller percentage of young people are being sexually solicited online than five years ago.

But children ages 10 to 17 are being increasingly bombarded with online porn and are being harassed and bullied more—often by peers, a study finds.

The long-awaited report, to be released today, is the only national study of its kind. It is by the University of New Hampshire's Crimes Against Children Research Center, which surveyed 1,500 children ages 10 to 17 last year and compared findings with a similar group five years earlier.

About 13% said in 2005 that they had received an unwanted request to engage in sexual activity or conversations in the previous year from either adults or other children. Five years earlier, it was 19%.

Though that's an improvement, it's "still way too high," says Ernie Allen, president of the National Center for Missing & Exploited Children. The center financed the research with a grant from Congress.

goal. Some Americans believe a combination of education and parental involvement is the most effective way to keep children safe online.

What's wrong with censoring the Internet to protect children? Firstly, strict laws tend to cast too wide a net. They don't distinguish between obscene or abusive content and informational or artistic content. For example, suppose a law restricted online content about breasts. Such a restriction could easily block public access to a wide swath of art, literature, and medical information—not to mention recipes for cooking chicken.

Allen and researcher David Finkelhor attribute improvements to education campaigns stressing "stranger danger" and less time spent in chat rooms "where creepy people hang out," Finkelhor says.

Many solicitations, 43%, were from others under age 18. And most of the time, children brushed them off. Aggressive solicitations, on the other hand, remained about the same.

Internet researcher Larry Rosen, a professor of psychology at California State University, Dominguez Hills, says the new research reinforces what he has seen: "There simply is not the volume of predators on MySpace that people imagine."

Children's exposure to porn comes despite increased supervision and use of filters. Also, five years ago, technology impeded the flow of graphic images; today, more people have high-speed access and fast computers, Finkelhor says.

The study found 9% of kids were "very upset" by seeing porn, up from 6% five years ago.

Finkelhor says more attention must be paid to online harassment. "We were concerned that not only were kids being harassed more, but they were doing more harassing."

Allen advocates a "three-pronged solution": education, enforcing existing laws and improving tools such as filters.

—Janet Kornblum

Strict laws are also constitutionally problematic. They censor communication among adults as well as among kids. The Supreme Court has repeatedly ruled that U.S. law should not pursue child protection so zealously that it reduces all communication to "that which would be suitable for a sandbox." Furthermore, even minors have free speech rights. Parents may constitutionally limit their children's speech, but the government may not.

Critics say that censorship laws could let parents off the hook in raising their children and put the government in charge. Instead of monitoring their children's online behavior, some parents might expect the government to do it for them. They might also blame digital media for family problems.

Meanwhile, critics say, Internet censorship offers only a fantasy of control. Censoring the Internet is both impossible and ineffective, they say. Because the Internet is ever changing and offers users a great deal of anonymity (the ability to hide one's identity), strict laws are difficult to enforce. And they miss prime targets because the Internet is international. Many Internet pornographers, for instance, are based in foreign countries. Thus they are beyond the reach of U.S. law.

Many Americans believe that policing mainly by parents and the Internet industry is more effective and more legally sound than government policing. Since no one can completely eliminate childhood cyberhazards, most children will eventually

encounter them. Parents and schools should therefore prepare children to be "citizens of the digital age." Children must learn to spot and cope safely with online dangers such as scams, predators, and bullying.

Research suggests that Internet education programs can help kids develop safer online habits. An example is the NCMEC NetSmartz program, which is designed to increase children's awareness of Internet dangers and to help them become more responsible Internet users. In 2005 graduate

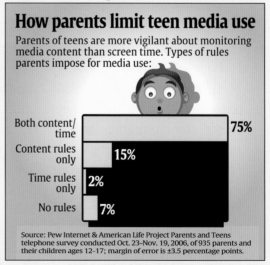

USA TODAY Snapshots®

How parents limit teen media use

Parents of teens are more vigilant about monitoring media content than screen time. Types of rules parents impose for media use:

Both content/time: 75%
Content rules only: 15%
Time rules only: 2%
No rules: 7%

Source: Pew Internet & American Life Project Parents and Teens telephone survey conducted Oct. 23-Nov. 19, 2006, of 935 parents and their children ages 12-17; margin of error is ±3.5 percentage points.

By Cindy Clark and Alejandro Gonzalez, USA TODAY, 2007

NetSmartz Evaluation

A 2005 survey of NetSmartz participants in Maine public schools showed that the program raised students' awareness of online hazards and how to use the Internet safely. The table below shows how the students' responses to key questions changed after the program.

Question	Preprogram Responses	Postprogram Responses
Is it safe to meet someone in person after chatting online for a long time?	46 percent of participants said no.	83 percent said no.
Is it safe to post your picture on the Internet?	75 percent said no.	96 percent said no.
Is it safe to tell people your real name on the Internet?	80 percent said no.	98 percent said no.
Is it safe to post your address on the Internet?	75 percent said no.	88 percent said no.

students at George Washington University evaluated the program and found it to be effective.

Research also shows that parents need to get more involved in their children's online activities. Another 2005 study showed that a majority of families have a computer in a low-traffic area, such as a bedroom or home office, which means that parents might not know when kids are online. About half of parents don't have—or don't know if they have—filtering or monitoring software. Most parents can't

www.usatoday.com

USA TODAY

News
SECTION A

July 2, 2008

Sexual predators prowl new outlet

From the Pages of
USA TODAY
Sexual predators are using gaming consoles such as the Wii, PlayStation and Xbox to meet children online.

"Child predators are migrating from traditional methods to alternate media," says Detective Lt. Thomas Kish of the Michigan State Police. "They are going to places where children are."

Predators view games that allow kids to access the Internet and text message other players as a "foot in the door," he says.

Parents may not realize that gaming consoles have become Internet devices or that savvy kids can bypass parental controls, says Marc Rogers, director of Purdue University's Cyber Forensics Lab in West Lafayette, Ind.

Police who have been doing stings in Internet chat rooms for years now are going undercover to catch predators playing interactive games, ranging from Grand Theft Auto to old-fashioned chess and checkers. They're making arrests.

In Utah, a man was charged this year with sexual exploitation of a minor for allegedly enticing a 12-year-old boy he met through an online game into having sex, says Lt. Jessica Farnsworth, field commander of the

decipher common chat room lingo, such as POS (parent over shoulder) and A/S/L (age/sex/location), so they might not know what their kids are talking about, even if they do monitor online behavior.

Meanwhile, evidence indicates that parental involvement improves childhood Internet safety. A 2006 study found that teens whose parents have talked to them "a lot" about online safety are less likely to have posted pictures of themselves on the Internet—often a lure for predators. The same teens are more likely to ignore or block messages from unfamiliar people and to report these occurrences to trusted adults.

The Family Online Safety Institute (FOSI), a nonprofit organization,

Utah Internet Crimes Against Children Task Force. She says predators meet kids on a game, "groom them and then try to move off the game."

In December, Michigan prosecutors convicted Adam Glenn Schroeder of criminal sexual conduct with a minor and using a computer to commit a crime. He used a game, World of Warcraft, to lure a 12-year-old girl into having sex with him. He was sentenced to 10 years in prison.

Police had found Schroeder on other games. "This guy had been doing it for a while," Kish says.

In another case, Kish says, a 10-year-old boy playing the Halo Xbox game got a video message from a man that showed the adult engaged in a sex act.

Farnsworth says her office has seized many Xbox machines for investigation and has received training from the maker, Microsoft, on how to extract text messages and other information from them.

Microsoft trains police at national conferences, says Tim Cranton, associate general counsel for the company's Worldwide Internet Safety Enforcement program.

Cranton says the Xbox has password-protected "family settings" that allow parents to turn off Internet access or track content and contacts. PlayStation and Wii also have such controls.

—Wendy Koch

supports the view that censorship is not the best way to keep children safe online. In 2009 FOSI made a recommendation to the FCC:

> The Commission should continue to encourage the use of advanced blocking technologies and other parental control solutions, without mandating a one-size-fits-all specific solution. The government can play an important role in protecting kids from inappropriate content online by encouraging additional research, funding educational efforts, and bringing together the online safety community to discuss this important issue.

CHAPTER FOUR
Public Morality

IN FEBRUARY 1998, SEVENTEEN-YEAR-OLD BRANDON Beussink created a website. On this site, he sharply criticized Woodland High School in Marble Hill, Missouri, where he was a junior. He lampooned school staff, using vulgar language to express his opinion about the principal, a teacher, and the school's website. Brandon invited readers to share their own opinions by e-mailing the principal. He provided a link to the school's site. However, he used his home computer outside school hours to create his site.

Another student with a grudge against Brandon showed the site to Delma Farrell, the lampooned teacher. The site upset Farrell, and she reported it to Yancy Poorman, the principal. Farrell demanded Poorman take action.

"When I viewed it and it was explained that it had been seen by other students, yes, sir, I

Left: Teens listen to a lecture on cyberbullying. As online speech has become more and more vulgar, many argue for stricter regulations.

was upset," said Poorman. He decided to act immediately. He suspended Brandon for ten days and told the student to clean up or delete the website. Poorman's discipline notice cited Brandon's "inappropriate comments," "slanderous remarks," "personal offenses to myself and Mrs. Farrell," the link to the school site, and abuse of school computers. Brandon took down his site later that day. But because of school policy regard-

arguing that Brandon's website had disrupted school operations. But Judge Rodney Sippel ruled in Brandon's favor. The judge said that Poorman had disciplined Brandon because the site had upset school officials, not because it had caused any substantial disruption at school. Sippel wrote, "Disliking or being upset by the content of a student's speech is not an acceptable justification for limiting student speech."

> " I think the school should practice what it teaches. We study history and we study the Constitution, but the school doesn't seem to think that applies to them. "
>
> —BRANDON BEUSSINK, 1998

ing absences, Brandon's grades all dropped to a failing level.

The following fall, Brandon sued the school district in federal court. In their defense, Woodland High School officials justified their actions by

The court said the school could not lower Brandon's grades because of his suspension-related absences. It also could not forbid Brandon to use his home computer for reposting his website.

State of the First Amendment
2008

State of the First Amendment is an annual survey conducted by researchers at the University of Connecticut. It examines public attitudes toward freedom of speech, press, and religion and toward the rights of assembly and petition. One survey question asked:

> The Federal Communications Commission is considering a proposal to provide free Internet access to anyone, anywhere in the United States. However, under the proposal, the government would block access to material it deemed indecent or obscene. Do you favor or oppose the FCC's proposal?

The answers broke down as follows:

Strongly favor	38 percent
Mildly favor	16 percent
Mildly disagree	12 percent
Strongly disagree	28 percent
Don't know/refuse	5 percent

Another question asked whether respondents agreed with the following statement: "People should be allowed to say things in public that might be offensive to [religious or racial] groups." The answers were as follows:

	Religious Groups	Racial Groups
Strongly agree	32 percent	24 percent
Mildly agree	23 percent	19 percent
Mildly disagree	12 percent	12 percent
Strongly disagree	30 percent	42 percent
Don't know/refuse	2 percent	2 percent

MORALITY ONLINE

Brandon Beussink's story illustrates another aspect of the debate over Internet censorship: public morality. Public morals—also called social norms—are a group's rules about appropriate and inappropriate values, beliefs, attitudes, and behaviors.

Some Americans want tighter public control over the Internet to preserve traditional, widely accepted customs and morals. These people believe that such customs and morals are vital to a civilized, peaceful society. They say that online obscenity, pornography, defamation, bigotry (hatred or intolerance of a particular group of people), and fighting words are offenses to traditional morals and values.

Other Americans say that laws cannot and should not control morality, because morals are relative. One person may think a particular act is wrong or bad, while another person believes the same act is right or good. Attempts to legislate morality often squash the free

Above: Internet content that offends some people is perfectly acceptable to others. Americans debate the extent to which laws should control this content.

Internet porn grows

One in four Internet users in the USA visited a pornography Web site this year.

Pornography Web sites

2000

88,000

2004

1.6 million

People who visit pornography Web sites

January 2002

27.5 million

May 2004

37 million

Sources: Websense Inc., 2004; Nielsen/Net Ratings, 2004.

By Bob Laird, USA TODAY, 2004

exchange of ideas, which is critical to democracy.

CIVILIZED SOCIETY NEEDS PROTECTION

Brandon Beussink broke the rules of public morality in more ways than one. He insulted authority figures. He harshly criticized an important community institution—his school. He used vulgar language—words that many people find disgusting and offensive. He encouraged others to follow his lead. Although the court sided with Brandon, many Americans supported the school's suspension of Brandon. They believe U.S. society should not tolerate online violations of public morality.

Some say that tolerating offensive Internet content sends the message that such content is socially acceptable. This acceptance in turn leads to more offensive behavior, both online and in other public venues. The ultimate result, many fear, is a turbulent society

> **"All of this raises the question, what should be done about this spread of hate through cyberspace? Most people, when they are presented with the scope of the problem say, 'There ought to be a law.'"**
>
> **—CHRISTOPHER WOLF,** INTERNET LAW EXPERT, 2000

lacking rules of conduct—a society in which people see no overarching need to respect others. The harsher the content, the more it worries the Internet's moral crusaders.

Websites that promote bigotry, such as white supremacy, offer some of the harshest content online. White supremacy is the belief that white people are superior to people of other racial backgrounds. White supremacists desire racial separation and white dominance in society and politics. They argue for "white power."

Some white supremacists believe violence is necessary to achieve their goals. Many have participated in murders and other violent crimes. For example, in 1999 white supremacist Benjamin Nathaniel Smith went on a shooting spree in Indiana and Illinois that left two dead and nine wounded. In 2009 white supremacist James W. von Brunn shot and killed a Holocaust museum guard in Washington, D.C.

Since the late 1990s, the white power movement has been working hard to attract supporters using sophisticated, user-friendly websites. "These groups use high technology to their advantage, and they don't look like monsters anymore. They look like average Americans," said Jack Levin in 1999. Levin is codirector of the Brudnick Center for the Study of Violence and Conflict at Northeastern University in Boston.

This trend has continued into the twenty-first century. According to the Southern Poverty Law Center (SPLC), which conducts tolerance education, fights hate groups in court, and tracks hate groups, the number of U.S. hate groups—mostly white supremacists—rose 54 percent from 2000 to 2009.

The renewed activity includes a boom on the Internet, says Don Black. Black is creator of the nation's largest white-power website, Stormfront. The site has more than 177,000 registered members. It carries heavy traffic, hosting up to 109,000 unique visitors per twenty-four-hour period. Black, a former leader of the Ku Klux Klan (a nearly 150-year-old white supremacist group), says he's encouraged by such enthusiasm. "We see a lot of people coming out of the woodwork," he says.

Experts don't believe the mere existence of hate websites can turn otherwise healthy, happy people into hateful bigots. Other factors, such as a tough economy and the election of Barack Obama, the first African American U.S. president, have also contributed to the rise of hate groups. But scholars and hate group leaders agree: the Internet is a very effective recruiting tool for hate groups. People who feel alienated and ignored can participate easily and anonymously—and feel as if they belong to something important and powerful.

History shows that gross violations of public morality online

Above: Don Black (pictured with his son Derek) uses his popular website Stormfront to spread controversial "white power" messages.

www.usatoday.com

USA TODAY

Life
SECTION D

April 26, 2000

Hate groups' Internet sites are grist for college course

From the Pages of
USA TODAY

Robert Hilliard, media arts professor at Emerson College in Boston and co-author of a book on hate groups and their savvy use of the media, especially the Internet, decided to bring the lesson to students in a course, Hate.com, that he's teaching this fall.

In his book, *Waves of Rancor: Tuning in the Radical Right*, "we showed how the extremist groups are using the Internet and radio" to get out the word—that they're planning a "racial holy war" and "genocide [mass murder of a racial, political, or cultural group]," Hilliard says.

There's no doubt the groups have used the Net effectively, he says. "The groups themselves have stated the Internet has opened up a whole new world for them. It has made it possible to reach out to millions of people, at little cost."

So you might think that Hilliard would support Internet companies that ban hate speech and that he'd call for the eradication of the groups on the Net. You'd be wrong. "We feel that our First Amendment is sacred to everybody."

Instead, Hilliard hopes that his students—most of whom will go into the media—will see these groups in their raw, uncensored form and draw their own conclusions. He has two goals with the course: to introduce students to what's happening, and to have them develop a strong opinion by the end of the course, then act on it with a specific project.

He also hopes other universities will follow with courses on hate. His 25-person class was quickly over-enrolled; he's considering a second class.

—Janet Kornblum

can be harmful—even deadly—to society. Hate sites raise the risk of violent crime by condoning violence. Some scholars say that Internet pornography harms women, children, and families by objectifying vulnerable people and commercializing sex. A

2007 survey investigated sex trafficking in four countries, including the United States. (Sex traffickers force girls and women to work as prostitutes, exchanging sex for money, and to appear in pornography.) The survey found that

> Internet pornography drives sex trafficking. . . . The anonymity of the Internet removes the element of social stigma attached to viewing pornography. Men are then, again through the anonymity of the Internet, able to search for and "purchase" deviant sex services anywhere in the world.

Pornography can also lead to harmful behavior among viewers. For example, the January 2008 *Journal of Adolescent Research* published a study of porn use among 813 college students. It showed a clear link between regular porn use and risky behaviors, such as binge drinking and having sex with multiple partners.

Given this evidence, why should the United States tolerate morally offensive online content? Wouldn't U.S. society be better off if it simply banned such content from the Internet?

DEMOCRACY NEEDS FREEDOM

No, say free speech advocates. They insist that a broad ban on offensive content would harm U.S. society far more than the content itself does. This argument rests on two main ideas. First: morals are not absolute, or one size fits all. Second: the free exchange of ideas—however repugnant some ideas may be—is critical to democracy.

Many believe that no single set of rules should dictate what is right and what is wrong. A single moral code is especially difficult to define in a large, diverse society such as the United States. Americans belong to many different faiths and cultures, and each one teaches a different set of rules. In any society, therefore, social norms can never really reflect right and wrong. Rather, they outline the basic beliefs most people share, or they simply reflect long-standing customs.

Craigslist eliminating erotic ad category: Sector has been called front for pornography, prostitution

From the Pages of USA TODAY

Online classified ads service Craigslist says it will dump the "erotic services" category that law enforcement officials have called a front for prostitution and replace it with a fee-based adult category that will be reviewed by site employees.

As of Wednesday, postings to the erotic category were no longer being accepted. In seven days, the category will be removed, Craigslist said. Postings on the adult category—which would seek to bar blatant ads for prostitution and pornography—will cost $10; once approved, they can be reposted for $5.

The sex-service listings have faced intense scrutiny following the death last month of a masseuse who advertised on Craigslist in Boston. Boston University student Philip Markoff, 23, was charged with the killing and with attacks on two other women he met through Craigslist. Tabloids called Markoff "the Craigslist killer."

That followed the sentencing last month of a Minnesota man convicted of killing a woman who replied to a babysitting ad on Craigslist.

"We're trying to strike a new balance for state attorneys general, legal businesses that advertise, advocates for free speech, and Internet law experts," Craigslist CEO Jim Buckmaster said in an interview.

The 14-year-old site generates more than 20 billion page views per month in 50 countries. Its listings cover everything from apartments to jobs.

The controversial erotic services category is one of 100 categories on Craigslist, and accounts for 1% of ads, Buckmaster says. The private San Francisco-based company does not comment on its revenue. Most ads on the site are posted without review.

In a lawsuit filed in March, Cook County (Ill.) Sheriff Tom Dart called the erotic category the "largest source of prostitution in America." Buckmaster called the lawsuit "baseless."

Above: At the online classified ad service Craigslist, executives try to balance free speech with community safety and morality.

Last week, the attorneys general of Illinois, Connecticut and Missouri met with Craigslist officials to put an end to what they claim were ads for illegal sexual activities. "Craigslist is doing the right thing in eliminating its online red light [district], but it hardly ends our concerns," Connecticut Attorney General Richard Blumenthal said in an interview. California AG [attorney general] Jerry Brown lauded the actions, but New York AG Andrew Cuomo called them "half-baked."

Craigslist made the move more as a public relations gesture than a legal one, free-speech advocates say. Under federal law, websites that host third-party material are "absolutely immune" from [criminal lawsuits], says Matt Zimmerman, an attorney at the Electronic Frontier Foundation, a non-profit that advocates free speech online.

But in its terms of service agreement, Craigslist has a "moral and legal responsibility" in its commitments to the public's safety, Blumenthal says.

—Jon Swartz

Individuals must ultimately decide for themselves what is right and wrong.

Censorship opponents say that a broad ban on offensive Internet content would be unjust. Such a ban would force the morals of some people on others who don't share the same beliefs. For example, Internet pornography offends many Americans. Religious leaders almost universally decry pornography. Many of their followers agree. Some scholars have found that porn use has harmful effects on society.

However, many Americans believe that adult use of pornography is naughty but harmless. And many researchers have found no negative effects on society from porn use. In fact, some studies suggest that sexual crimes decrease when pornography is more widely available.

How can U.S. society handle such a clash of beliefs and data? Recent history shows that censorship laws are not a workable solution. USA TODAY writer Joan Biskupic points out, "For years, Congress has sought what amounts to a legislative Holy Grail [ideal]: A law that would protect children from Internet pornography, stay relevant in the face of evolving technology, and not be too much of a restriction for adults who want to exercise their constitutional right to view sexually explicit materials."

But Congress has failed in every attempt to create such a law. And the Supreme Court has indicated that further attempts to regulate Internet pornography (except for child pornography, which almost all Americans agree is harmful) would be futile. Many people say that families, not the government, must protect children from online porn and other harmful content. Further, the Supreme Court believes that any government effort to widely limit explicit materials on the Web is unconstitutional. Justice Anthony Kennedy explained, "Content-based prohibitions . . . have the constant potential to be a repressive force in the lives and thoughts of a free people."

Why is it so important for Americans to communicate—online and elsewhere—with absolute freedom? Free-speech advocates say that without the freedoms of speech, press, religion, assembly, and petition guaranteed by the First Amendment, democracy could not exist. Without the protection of these freedoms, the government could establish a national religion, persecute religious minorities, silence protesters, and muzzle members of the press who criticized the government. Citizens could not mobilize for social change. Judge Sippel summarized this concept eloquently in his 1998 opinion on *Beussink v. Woodland R-IV School.* He wrote,

> Indeed, it is provocative and challenging speech, like Beussink's, which is most in need of the protections of the First Amendment. Popular speech is not likely to provoke censure [condemnation]. It is unpopular speech that invites censure. It is unpopular speech which needs the protection of the First Amendment. The First Amendment was designed for this very purpose.

CHAPTER FIVE

Security

IN FEBRUARY 2005, THE FEDERAL BUREAU OF INVESTI-gation (FBI) office in New Haven, Connecticut, received an e-mail that looked like a terrorist threat. FBI agents suspected the message was a prank but believed they had to investigate it.

The e-mail's sender had used an Internet service provided by the Library Connection, a group of Connecticut public libraries. The FBI demanded that the Library Connection hand over the sender's real name, street address, and Internet usage logs. To make this demand, an FBI agent delivered a national security letter to the Library Connection.

A national security letter is a written legal command. It requires a business or organization to produce client records. These records may include:

- Internet and telephone data, such as names, addresses, log-on times, e-mail addresses, and names of service providers

Left: Teenagers use computers at a public library in the early 2000s.

- Financial records, such as bank statements
- Credit information, such as loan and mortgage statements

Unlike search warrants and court orders, a national security letter does not need approval by a judge or a jury. A local FBI official simply certifies that the information sought by the national security letter is relevant to a foreign intelligence or international terrorism investigation. In addition, national security letters come with a gag order. They forbid recipients to discuss the demands with anyone but their lawyers.

The Library Connection refused to hand over its records. Instead, it filed a lawsuit in a federal court. The lawsuit claimed that national security letters are unconstitutional because they violate the right to privacy. If citizens fear they're being monitored or disclosing private information when they use the Internet, they won't speak freely online. This violation of privacy is thus a violation of free speech.

SECURITY AND PRIVACY: CAN THEY COEXIST?

The e-mail threat to Connecticut's FBI did turn out to be a hoax. But the subsequent lawsuit sparked an important public debate.

Americans generally agree that security should be a national priority. They acknowledge that some people—both at home and abroad—would like to create mayhem in the United States. The Internet is a useful tool for terrorists. They can use it to spread political messages, recruit followers, share information about weapons, find weaknesses in U.S. security, steal information, announce threats, and harass individuals or organizations. In response, government officials can also track troublemakers' online activities in an effort to prevent such mayhem.

While they want security, Americans generally agree that privacy is critical to democracy. Lack of privacy is a form of censorship. People will not speak freely if they fear their words are being monitored. Most citizens don't want to give the government easy access to personal records or a broad ability to monitor their online activities.

Security and privacy are, to some extent, competing goals. U.S. society struggles to balance them. The editors of *USA TODAY* framed this debate in a June 2008 editorial. They wrote: "The question has never been whether terrorists are a threat to this nation (they are) or whether U.S. intelligence officials should be able to spy aggressively on them (they should). It's how to achieve those ends without trading away the privacy of Americans."

SAFETY FIRST

Some Americans believe that the government should do as much as it can to keep citizens safe. They don't mind trading some privacy for a potentially safer country. This view gained many supporters after the September 11 terrorist attacks.

In response to these attacks, the U.S. government enacted two measures aimed at preventing additional terrorist attacks in the United States and abroad. Both affected online speech. The first measure was an executive order by President George W. Bush called the President's Surveillance Program. This program allows government intelligence agents to secretly monitor electronic communications originating abroad (phone calls, e-mails, Internet activity, text messaging, and faxes) to or from anyone suspected of terrorist

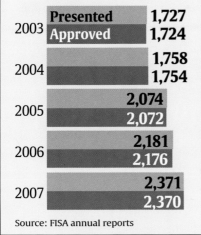

Compliant court

In the past five years, the Foreign Intelligence Surveillance Court has approved nearly all applications for electronic surveillance and physical searches.

	Presented	Approved
2003	1,727	1,724
2004	1,758	1,754
2005	2,074	2,072
2006	2,181	2,176
2007	2,371	2,370

Source: FISA annual reports

By Julie Snider, USA TODAY, 2008

links—even if one party in the communication is in the United States. Because this monitoring requires no court-approved search warrant, Americans commonly call it warrantless wiretapping.

The other measure was the USA PATRIOT Act, passed on October 26, 2001. Among other things, the PATRIOT Act gave law enforcement agencies more power to search telephone, e-mail, medical, financial, and other records. The PATRIOT Act also eased restrictions on spying within the United States. And the act expanded the definition of the word *terrorism* to include U.S.-based terrorism.

The PATRIOT Act had a big impact on national security letters. Congress had first approved the letters in 1986,

Above: President George W. Bush signs the USA PATRIOT Act on October 26, 2001. The law assigns greater powers to law enforcement, but many people say it tramples on the First Amendment.

> ## " If there's information on a potential terrorist that can help, wouldn't you want [the FBI] to have it? "
>
> — **KEVIN O'CONNOR,** U.S. ATTORNEY FOR CONNECTICUT, 2006
>
> **USA TODAY · JULY 6, 2006**

but only high-ranking FBI officials could authorize the letters. And the FBI could use national security letters only for pursuing foreign spies. The PATRIOT Act expanded the letters' reach. Under the act, lower-ranking officials could authorize the letters—and could use them for many more purposes.

With this change came an increase in usage. According to U.S. Department of Justice figures, the FBI served eighty-five hundred national security letters in 2000. The number had nearly tripled by 2008. That year the FBI served almost twenty-five thousand letters. Usage peaked at forty-seven thousand letters in 2005.

Among the tens of thousands of national security letters issued from 2001 to 2009, only three have faced legal challenges. The vast majority of letters remain secret. Recipients of the letters are forbidden to talk about them in almost all cases. Government officials insist that the letters must stay secret to keep targets from learning that they are being watched. And federal agencies carefully guard the information they collect.

This secrecy makes it impossible for the public to know how effective the letters are. The government assures Americans that the letters are necessary for national security. The FBI says they're vital to disrupting terrorist plots and other national security threats before attacks occur. Kevin O'Connor, the U.S. attorney for Connecticut, stresses that the government was only trying to keep people safe in the Library Connection case.

"All we wanted was identifying information," he said. "God forbid it [wasn't] a hoax."

Secrecy surrounds the U.S. government's warrantless wiretapping activities too. Many people doubt their effectiveness, but government officials support these activities with passion.

In early 2008, President Bush demanded quick passage of a law renewing warrantless wiretapping. He said this law was vital because "terrorists are planning attacks on our country...that will make September 11 pale by comparison." Bush said the law would let the government "quickly and effectively monitor the plans of terrorists outside the USA, while respecting" civil liberties.

Kit Bond, vice chairman of the U.S. Senate Select Committee on Intelligence, backed up Bush. "As numerous courts have affirmed, our Constitution gives the president authority to engage in surveillance of foreign terrorists," he said. After the U.S. House of Representatives passed the bill, Bond urged his fellow senators to follow suit: "The House ultimately did the right thing in passing this bill; the Senate should, too." The Senate did.

CHECKS AND BALANCES

Many Americans strongly oppose warrantless wiretapping, national security letters, and other broad surveillance (spying) measures. They agree that the U.S. government has a responsibility to protect its

> **They who can give up essential liberty to obtain a little temporary safety, deserve neither liberty nor safety.**
>
> **—BENJAMIN FRANKLIN,** 1775

Above: The FBI (headquartered in the building above in Washington, D.C.) needs strong laws to protect the nation from terrorism. But how strong is too strong?

citizens. They acknowledge that secret surveillance and investigation are sometimes necessary. But they decry the use of such tactics without checks and balances.

Checks and balances are a key element of democracy. Each branch of U.S. government can limit the acts of the other two branches. This system prevents any one branch from becoming too powerful. It also encourages the branches to cooperate with one another. Opponents believe that with warrantless wiretapping and national security letters, the executive branch is acting without checks and balances from the judicial branch.

Commercial satellites alter global security

From the Pages of
USA TODAY

The secretive National Geospatial-Intelligence Agency is rushing to get the latest, high-definition satellite photos of Afghanistan into the hands of U.S. ground troops as they ramp up operations in the country's tangled terrain.

The NGA analysts aren't tapping the government's huge network of highly classified spy satellites; they're getting the pictures from commercial vendors. That's the same stuff pretty much anyone can get, either through free, online programs, such as Google Earth, or by buying it from the same companies supplying Uncle Sam.

It's a remarkable turn, given the warnings that security experts in the USA and worldwide raised a few years ago about giving the entire planet—terrorists and rogue states included—access to high-resolution satellite photos once available only to superpowers.

Last month, the most powerful commercial satellite in history sent its first pictures back to Earth, and another with similar capabilities is set for launch in mid-2009. The imagery provided by those and other commercial satellites has transformed global security in fundamental ways, forcing even the most powerful nations to hide facilities and activities that are visible not only to rival nations, but even to their own citizens.

In August 2006, the Islamic Army in Iraq circulated an instructional video on how to aim rockets at U.S. military sites using Google Earth.

Posted on a jihadist [radical Islamist] website, the video showed a computer using the program to zoom in for close-up views of buildings at Iraq's Rasheed Airport, according to an unclassified U.S. intelligence report obtained by USA TODAY. The segment ended with the caption, "Islamic Army in Iraq/The Military Engineering Unit—Preparations for Rocket Attack."

The video appeared to fulfill the dire predictions raised by security experts in the USA and across the globe when Google began offering free Internet access to worldwide satellite imagery in 2005. Officials in countries as diverse as Australia, India, Israel and the Netherlands complained publicly that it would be a boon to terrorists and hostile states, especially since the pictures often provide a site's map coordinates.

Indeed, some terrorist attacks have been planned with the help of Google Earth, including an event in 2006 in which terrorists used car bombs in an unsuccessful effort to destroy oil facilities in Yemen, according to Yemeni press reports. Images from Google Earth and other commercial sources have been found in safe houses used by al-Qaeda and other terror groups, according to the Pentagon.

The world's governments have taken a variety of steps in response to the emergence of Google Earth and other commercial imagery sources, according to a confidential report issued in July by the CIA's Open Source Center and made public by the Federation of American Scientists. Among them:

- *Negotiation*. Some nations have asked Google and other companies to keep certain images off the market, the report says. For example, Google Earth uses older imagery of parts of Iraq based on British concerns about exposing military sites. Commercial satellite companies often blur images of sensitive U.S. sites, such as the Pentagon.
- *Bans*. China has barred websites selling "unapproved" commercial imagery, according to the report, and Sudan has banned Google Earth. In 2006, Bahrain officials banned Google Earth, but the CIA report notes that the move may have been mainly to "prevent exposure of elaborate residences and land holdings of the country's rich."
- *Evasion*. Many countries have stepped up efforts to conceal sensitive facilities, either by putting them underground or camouflaging them, the report says. Others, such as India, have improved their ability to discern when satellites pass overhead, which allows them to conduct sensitive military activities when cameras aren't watching.

"We actively engage with organizations and governments . . . to strike a balance between their security concerns and the needs of the end user," says Chikai Ohazama, Google Earth's product management director. Sensitive sites often are obscured by satellite operators before Google even gets the imagery, he adds. It often doesn't matter "because the imagery already is available from other places."

—Peter Eisler

Letting intelligence agencies act without judicial oversight "is an open invitation to perform fishing expeditions [open-ended, unjustified investigations]" that trample individual privacy rights, said Ann Beeson, a lawyer for Connecticut's Library Connection. Under the PATRIOT Act, agents can spy on individuals who are not targets of security investigations. This means the FBI is free to gather "sensitive information about innocent people."

Because the PATRIOT Act and the PSP are constitutionally problematic and because the executive branch has not yet provided convincing evidence that these programs work, many Americans want them changed. From 2001 to 2009, Americans tried to investigate and change the policies via lawsuits and legislation. But little progress was made.

Above: When librarians protested in 2004 against the PATRIOT Act, U.S. Attorney General John Ashcroft accused them of "baseless hysteria." Librarians countered with more appeals to protect freedom of speech.

Internet Censorship around the World

All nations implement some level of Internet censorship. In the United States, for instance, schools and libraries must use filters to block access to pornography. But in some nations, Internet censorship is pervasive. These countries block all political dissent, political discussions, sexual content, and anything else that might be seen as controversial, offensive, or threatening to the government. Many of these nations also have extremely repressive governments, with widespread denial of civil liberties. Reporters without Borders, a press freedom group, calls the following nations Internet Enemies:

- Burma (also called Myanmar)
- China
- Cuba
- Egypt
- Iran
- North Korea

- Saudi Arabia
- Syria
- Tunisia
- Uzbekistan
- Vietnam

Above: A police officer patrols an Internet café in China in 2006. In China Internet censorship is pervasive.

Senate OKs surveillance revamp

From the Pages of
USA TODAY

The Senate approved a major revision of the 30-year-old law regulating the government's electronic surveillance program Wednesday, ending a debate that threatened to freeze intelligence operations.

[President] Bush said the bill will allow the government "to quickly and effectively monitor the plans of terrorists outside the USA, while respecting" civil liberties.

Congress faced pressure to pass the bill because wiretaps granted under interim legislation were to expire in August. If new orders had to be obtained, ongoing operations could have been delayed.

The bill will give a secret court the power to supervise the administration's warrantless surveillance program, which was launched after 9/11 to hunt terrorists.

Opponents said the bill codifies an unconstitutional program. The American Civil Liberties Union and the Electronic Frontier Foundation vowed a court challenge.

"This program broke the law, and this president broke the law," said Sen. Russ Feingold, D-Wis., a leading opponent. Senators will regret they passed the law if they learn more about the program, he said.

Bush authorized warrantless intercepts of international calls between suspected terrorists abroad and people in the USA soon after the Sept. 11, 2001, terrorist attacks.

Warrants for such surveillance typically must be approved by a special court created by the Foreign Intelligence Surveillance Act (FISA) of 1978, which aimed to better regulate surveillance of foreign spies or terrorists operating in the USA.

The 1978 law was passed after revelations of domestic spying by the FBI and CIA [Central Intelligence Agency].

After the *New York Times* revealed the warrantless surveillance program in 2005, Bush agreed to place the program under the FISA court's supervision.

—Peter Eisler

In September 2009, a group of U.S. senators led by Russ Feingold and Dick Durbin proposed the Judicious Use of Surveillance Tools in Counter-terrorism Efforts (JUSTICE) Act. Instead of revising the problematic PATRIOT Act and PSP laws, the JUSTICE Act would replace them. It would introduce stronger safeguards and higher standards of judicial oversight for surveillance activity. Introducing this bill to the Senate, Feingold said:

> The JUSTICE Act . . . takes a comprehensive approach to fixing the Patriot Act and the FISA Amendments Act [a 2008 law formalizing the PSP], once and for all. It permits the government to conduct necessary surveillance, but within a framework of accountability and oversight. It ensures both that our government has the tools to keep us safe, and that the privacy and civil liberties of innocent Americans will be protected. Because we can and must do both. These are not mutually exclusive goals.

CHAPTER SIX

Intellectual Property

DMITRY SKLYAROV WAS A PHD STUDENT AND a computer programmer for the Russian software company ElcomSoft. He lived and worked in Moscow, Russia. But for five months in late 2001, the twenty-seven-year-old was trapped in the United States.

With Sklyarov's help, ElcomSoft had created a software product called the Advanced e-Book Processor (AEBP). The AEBP translated e-books (electronic books) from the Adobe e-book format to Portable Document Format (PDF). This translation removed electronic locks that publishers can put on e-books. Such locks can prevent users from copying and printing text and converting text to speech.

Left: Russian computer programmer Dmitry Sklyarov faced charges in 2001 for violating the Digital Millennium Copyright Act. He had created software that allowed users to bypass electronic locks on digital books.

By removing such restrictions, the AEBP let people who bought e-books use them in various ways. With the AEBP, an e-book buyer could, for example:

- Read the e-book on a device other than the one on which he or she had first downloaded it
- Still read the e-book after the device for which it was purchased had become unusable
- Print the e-book on paper
- Copy snippets of an e-book to quote in a school project, a critique, academic research, or a parody
- Have a computer read an e-book out loud (a common need among visually impaired people)

All of these uses were legal. They qualified as fair use. This legal doctrine says that portions of copyrighted materials may be used without permission of the copyright owner, provided such use does not interfere with the copyright owner's profits.

In July 2001, Sklyarov spoke at a computer conference in Las Vegas, Nevada. Federal law enforcement agents arrested him there. They charged Sklyarov and ElcomSoft with selling illegal software in the United States.

What was illegal about the AEBP? It violated the 1998 Digital Millennium Copyright Act (DMCA). Lawmakers had passed the DMCA to help prevent online piracy—the illegal reproduction of copyrighted digital material, including electronic text, images, audio and video files, and software.

Neither Sklyarov nor his employer had engaged in piracy. That is, they had not actually illegally reproduced any copyrighted digital materials. But the DMCA also makes it illegal to manufacture, sell, distribute, or use any technology that people *might use* to circumvent, or bypass, electronic locks. Therefore, the AEBP was illegal under the DMCA.

DMCA Highlights

Among other things, the Digital Millennium Copyright Act of 1998 *(shown below)*:

- Makes it a crime to bypass electronic antipiracy measures
- Outlaws the manufacture, sale, or distribution of code-cracking devices used to illegally copy software
- Permits electronic lock picking to conduct research on electronic locks, evaluate product performance, and test computer security systems
- Permits nonprofit libraries, archives, and educational institutions to temporarily bypass electronic antipiracy measures in deciding whether to in-clude works in their collections, but only when no other means of evaluation is available
- Limits legal liability for ISPs that may unknowingly transmit illegal material
- Requires ISPs to remove material that appears to violate copyright laws from users' websites

---

THE DIGITAL MILLENNIUM COPYRIGHT ACT OF 1998
U.S. Copyright Office Summary

December 1998

INTRODUCTION

The Digital Millennium Copyright Act (DMCA)[1] was signed into law by President Clinton on October 28, 1998. The legislation implements two 1996 World Intellectual Property Organization (WIPO) treaties: the WIPO Copyright Treaty and the WIPO Performances and Phonograms Treaty. The DMCA also addresses a number of other significant copyright-related issues.

The DMCA is divided into five titles:

- Title I, the **"WIPO Copyright and Performances and Phonograms Treaties Implementation Act of 1998,"** implements the WIPO treaties.
- Title II, the **"Online Copyright Infringement Liability Limitation Act,"** creates limitations on the liability of online service providers for copyright infringement when engaging in certain types of activities.
- Title III, the **"Computer Maintenance Competition Assurance Act,"** creates an exemption for making a copy of a computer program by activating a computer for purposes of maintenance or repair.
- Title IV contains six **miscellaneous provisions**, relating to the functions of the Copyright Office, distance education, the exceptions in the Copyright Act for libraries and for making ephemeral recordings, "webcasting" of sound recordings on the Internet, and the applicability of collective bargaining agreement obligations in the case of transfers of rights in motion pictures.
- Title V, the **"Vessel Hull Design Protection Act,"** creates a new form of protection for the design of vessel hulls.

This memorandum summarizes briefly each title of the DMCA. It provides merely an overview of the law's provisions; for purposes of length and readability a significant amount of detail has been omitted. **A complete understanding of any provision of the DMCA requires reference to the text of the legislation itself.**

---

[1]Pub. L. No. 105-304, 112 Stat. 2860 (Oct. 28, 1998).

Copyright Office Summary   *December 1998*   Page 1

Was Sklyarov's arrest fair? Is the DMCA a just law? These questions represent a broader debate in U.S. society.

IDEAS AS PROPERTY

In a short time, the Internet has profoundly changed the way people share ideas with one another. As a result, Americans are grappling with a new question: Can ideas be property? And if so, how should U.S. law treat this property?

For thousands of years, humans shared information with one another on a personal level. They told stories, sang songs, and crafted artworks and useful objects. They had no way to reproduce these works on a large scale. Nor did they recognize the right of humans to own their ideas. Ideas simply passed through people on the way to other people. People thought only physical items could be property that could be owned.

Then the printing press came along. So did factories, photographs, sound recordings, moving pictures, computers, and a host of other technological developments. Technology enabled people to make many copies of the art, literature, and other ideas they had dreamed up. As a result, society began to see these intellectual works as "property."

People developed copyright and patent laws to protect

> **"If you have an apple and I have an apple and we exchange these apples then you and I will still each have one apple. But if you have an idea and I have an idea and we exchange these ideas, then each of us will have two ideas."**
>
> —**GEORGE BERNARD SHAW,** DATE UNKNOWN

> ❝ **If nature has made any one thing less susceptible than all others of exclusive property, it is the action of the thinking power called an idea.** ❞

—**THOMAS JEFFERSON,** 1813

intellectual property owners. These laws give authors, inventors, and artists some control over their work. Other people must pay them to use or reproduce the work. Paying creators not only provides them with money but also encourages the flow of ideas.

Historically, copyright and patent laws have focused not on ideas themselves but on the physical expression of ideas. Physical expression is the way ideas take shape as objects, such as books, paintings, films, or gadgets. Copyright and patent laws, like other property laws, define property as physical items. According to the U.S. Copyright Office, copyright protects a particular expression of ideas or facts. It does not protect the ideas or facts themselves.

DIGITAL DILEMMA

How do computers and the Internet change this system? They offer a new and drastically different way of sharing and storing information.

People are rapidly digitizing as much information as they can. That is, they are changing the intellectual expressions once stored in fixed objects, such as books and filmstrips, into electrical patterns darting around the Internet. We can behold these expressions as glowing pixels (points of light that combine to create an image) or as transmitted sounds, but we cannot touch, hold, or own them in a traditional sense.

Digital technology removes information from the physical world, and societies are trying to write laws that govern the sharing of such nonphysical information. During the 1990s and early 2000s, U.S. lawmakers wrote new laws for electronic information sharing based upon old laws that define property in physical terms. This approach has proved problematic.

John Perry Barlow cofounded the Electronic Frontier Foundation (EFF), a civil liberties group. He is also a retired cattle rancher and former songwriter for the rock band the Grateful Dead—and thus the owner of many valuable copyrights. In his essay "The Economy of Ideas," Barlow eloquently describes the dilemma that digital intellectual property presents:

> If our property can be infinitely reproduced and instantaneously distributed all over the planet without cost, without

Above: John Perry Barlow—founder of the Electronic Frontier Foundation—believes we need new kinds of copyright laws to govern the world of online speech.

our knowledge, without its even leaving our possession, how can we protect it? How are we going to get paid for the work we do with our minds? And, if we can't get paid, what will assure the continued creation and distribution of such work? . . .

Furthermore . . . when the primary articles of commerce in a society look so much like speech as to be indistinguishable from it, and when the traditional methods of protecting their ownership have become ineffectual, attempting to fix the problem with broader and more vigorous enforcement will inevitably threaten freedom of speech. The greatest constraint on your future liberties may come not from government but from corporate legal departments laboring to protect by force [lawsuits] what can no longer be protected by practical efficiency or general social consent.

> **If our property can be infinitely reproduced and instantaneously distributed all over the planet without cost, without our knowledge, without its even leaving our possession, how can we protect it? How are we going to get paid for the work we do with our minds? And, if we can't get paid, what will assure the continued creation and distribution of such work?**
>
> **—JOHN PERRY BARLOW,** GRATEFUL DEAD SONGWRITER AND COFOUNDER OF THE ELECTRONIC FRONTIER FOUNDATION, 1994

As an artist himself, Barlow understands and appreciates the purpose copyright laws serve. They work well for protecting intellectual expressions that are physical. But Barlow believes these laws are becoming ineffective, because intellectual expressions are becoming increasingly electronic. They are growing more and more like pure thought. Barlow says that trying to control the sharing of digital information in the same way we control the sharing of physical information is a threat to free speech. This approach creates an environment in which people constantly fear lawsuits and restrict their creative, academic, commercial, and other activities to avoid legal trouble.

A society that values creativity and innovation must somehow reward its thinkers—writers, artists, inventors, and so on—for their efforts. Historically, U.S. society has rewarded its thinkers by paying them and by enacting laws that control public access to their works. Some Americans argue that electronic information must be protected the same way. They support electronic locks on digital intellectual properties, as well as laws such as the DMCA that prevent people from "picking" the locks.

But other Americans disagree. They say that locking up electronic information equates to censorship. They say that because digital information is so different from physical expressions of information, restricting its flow actually hinders the free exchange of ideas, putting both social progress and democracy in peril.

A NECESSARY COMPROMISE

In the early twenty-first century, intellectual property protectionists have the upper hand. The DMCA is already on the books. And this law has centuries of history and habit behind it.

The DMCA's strongest supporters are people involved in the publishing, entertainment, and software industries. Supporters believe that the DMCA is a necessary and fair compromise between the needs of consumers and the needs of creators. Their argument is largely economic.

DMCA supporters believe that financial reward is a key incentive for human creativity and innovation. Writers, artists, programmers, and other innovators typically earn their pay from publishers, recording studios, film companies, and so on. But such industries will not be able to pay creators without protection from piracy.

Suppose a film studio spends $100 million producing one feature-length movie. This price tag includes, among many other things, payment for the work of creative people such as screenwriters, actors, composers, musicians, and costume and set designers. If—without permission and without paying the studio—people copy and resell or give away the movie using an electronic device, the movie studio will lose the profits it would have made selling the movie on its own. Why would a film studio keep creating movies if people could easily copy them for free? The studios would lose money and go out of business.

The same goes for music recording companies, book

Film studios such as Walt Disney Pictures (above), recording companies, book publishers, and others have a strong financial interest in stopping and punishing online pirates.

publishers, computer software companies, and so on. The publishing, software, and entertainment industries fear that people will steal their books, programs, films, TV shows, and songs. In this view, people who pick digital locks are like consumers who rent a product and then refuse to return it.

ONLINE PIRATES

One common way to bypass digital copyright protections is peer-to-peer (P2P) file sharing. On a P2P network, any computer can exchange digital files (documents, music, videos, software, and so on) directly with any other computer in the network. Individuals in a P2P network need not use e-mail or transmit the files through a central computer server. Network members can offer any files they want to others and can, in turn, download any files made available by other members.

The first widely known file-sharing service was Napster, which operated from 1999 to 2001. Napster helped millions of users share files—mostly music—for free, bypassing the retail music market. (A central computer kept track of which users had which files, so Napster wasn't a true peer-to-peer system.) The Recording Industry Association of America (RIAA) accused Napster of massive copyright violations. A high-profile DMCA lawsuit ensued. In 2001 a court order shut down Napster's service. The company soon went bankrupt.

Computer programmers and file sharers learned a lesson from Napster's failure. They developed P2P software that let users exchange files without a central server. Decentralized P2P is difficult to monitor and control. Many P2P sites operate illegally.

During the Napster days, legal media-sharing sites didn't exist. A decade later, such sites are gaining popularity. They stream (broadcast via the Internet) or let users download digital files in ways that generate income for copyright owners. For example, iTunes charges a small fee for each song, video, or other file downloaded. Hulu streams

Above: Services such as iTunes allow users to legally download music from the Internet—usually for a small fee.

favorite television programs and movies with advertising, and advertisers pay copyright owners. In 2008 a study showed that among Internet users who downloaded digital media, roughly half used legal services.

But the other half of digital media seekers in 2008 used illegal P2P services. In 2009 a P2P monitoring company reported more than 1.5 billion P2P searches per day. The publishing, entertainment, and software industries say that only strong laws such as the DMCA can give some financial protection to copyright owners.

10 years after Napster, online pirates alive and well

<u>From the Pages of</u>
<u>USA TODAY</u>

A file-sharing fine against a Minnesota woman that mushroomed from $220,000 to nearly $2 million last week is just the latest evidence that illegally trading music and videos online is still with us in a big way.

In the spring, while pirates off the coast of Somalia were getting all the high-seas attention, four Swedish pirates of a totally different sort were being sentenced to pay more than $3 million in fines and serve a year in the brig. Their crime: running The Pirate Bay, one of the Web's most-visited file-sharing communities.

The Pirate Bay is part of the trend of peer-to-peer technologies used to illegally swap music, videos and applications. Public sites such as Pirate Bay, IsoHunt and Mininova index and track BitTorrent files, which allow computers to connect and download content. People go to these sites to search for and grab music or videos.

Private "torrent" communities, such as PassThePopcorn.org, What.cd and Waffles.fm are so popular that there are many websites devoted solely to gaining entry to these cyberguilds. What.cd, for instance, has more than 96,000 registered users.

The legal ramifications of peer-to-peer file-sharing are still being worked out, but copyright infringement is a crime. Anyone who widely distributes copyrighted material runs a risk of being fined—or worse. Part of the appeal of peer-to-peer file-sharing is that it is difficult to shut down because pirated files are never kept on a single server that can easily be targeted by law enforcement.

While The Pirate Bay and other public sites get the most news coverage, the momentum now is toward the private torrent communities: Websites that are accessible by invitation only, have strict rules about sharing and etiquette and usually focus on a single type of pirated content, such as music or films.

PassThePopcorn.org, as the name implies, tracks only files for downloading films but offers everything from the lowest resolutions all the way up to the high-definition quality available on Blu-ray discs. To join, you have to be invited by a current member.

The What.cd community, operating on a similar model, shares more than 270,000 musical albums representing 140,000 bands, according to internal statistics posted on its website.

Mike Masnick, CEO of research firm Techdirt, say that while private BitTorrent trackers are proliferating, it is difficult to directly assess this growth. Shrouded in secrecy, private trackers are illegal and try not to attract attention.

In a widely publicized incident in 2007, private community Oink. cd—whose members famously included Nine Inch Nails frontman Trent Reznor—was raided by international police organization Interpol, and a few of its members were charged with copyright infringement.

It's been 10 years since the original Napster was launched, ushering in the concept of picking up songs, TV shows and movies for free via online uploads and downloads.

And despite growing popularity of legal media sites such as iTunes, Hulu and Rhapsody, worldwide media piracy still looms large.

Scott Harrer, brand director at P2P intelligence and security firm Tiversa, said his company monitors more than 1.5 billion peer-to-peer searches a day, up from 500 million just one year ago.

Still, Recording Industry Association of America spokesman Jonathan Lamy says the tide is starting to turn, just a bit. He points to a recent study by market tracker NPD Group showing that in 2008, 18% of Internet users downloaded music or other media from a pirate site, compared with 22% who opted for a legitimate site.

The RIAA, which has initiated copyright-infringement legal action against 35,000 individuals, is no longer actively suing folks for unauthorized music sharing online.

Despite its big Minnesota win, it now prefers to work directly with Internet service providers to get its message out, via warning letters and more.

Lamy won't say which ISPs the RIAA is partnering with. But he says that now someone engaging in file-sharing would simply be dropped by the ISP rather than sued.

Karl Bode, editor of Broadbandreports.com, doesn't think such approaches will work: "I've seen every attempt in the book to reduce peer-to-peer piracy, but it just continues to grow."

—Russ Juskalian

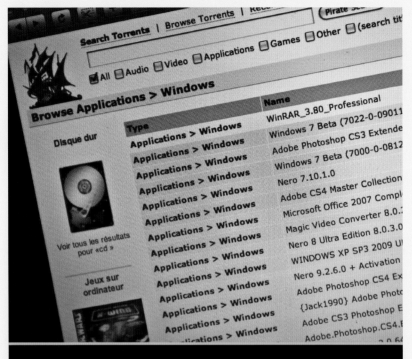

Above: Websites such as the Pirate Bay have followed in the footsteps of Napster. Movie studios and recording companies want to see these sites shut down.

NOTICE AND TAKEDOWN

Not only does the DMCA protect creators and businesses from piracy, it also provides liability protection (protection against legal penalties) to online intermediaries. ISPs are one example of online intermediaries. Other examples are hosts of interactive websites—such as blogs, social networking sites such as Facebook, video-sharing sites such as YouTube, and wiki sites (collaborative websites) such as Wikipedia.

Internet users sometimes post copyrighted material online illegally. The DMCA protects intermediaries from being sued for hosting such illegal posts. To earn that protection, the intermediary must promptly remove material if a copyright owner sends a "takedown" notice. The intermediary can restore the material only if the user who posted it certifies that it's being used legally and if the copyright owner does not pursue the claim in court.

Online intermediaries tend to resist innovation and restrict access to their services when they fear lawsuits. The DMCA removed this fear. Internet-based businesses say that the DMCA's notice-and-takedown provision opened vast opportunities in both public dialogue and business. In 1998 interactive websites were nearly unheard of. A decade later, they are thriving. Some, such as Google, are among the world's largest companies.

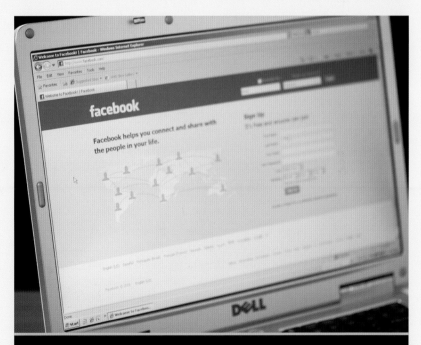

Above: Interactive websites such as Facebook are protected from liability under the DMCA. This means that if their users post copyrighted material, the sites cannot be sued for copyright infringement.

Sky-high sales for U2's 'Horizon' debut

From the Pages of USA TODAY

U2's *No Line on the Horizon* takes a vertical leap to No. 1 on Billboard's album chart after selling 484,000 copies its first week, the biggest opener since Britney Spears' *Circus* sold 505,000 in early December.

Though lower than U2's last studio disc, sales for the band's 12th album and seventh chart-topper met expectations, says Keith Caulfield, Billboard's senior chart analyst.

Despite a lukewarm reception to single Get on Your Boots, Caulfield expects *Horizon* to enjoy "a long chart life and long shelf life. There will be endless singles. They've got a big tour coming. U2 is a no-brainer."

Few doubt that piracy, a plague on all album sales (down 11.5% this year compared to 2008), siphoned profits from *Horizon*, which leaked online 13 days early. It was downloaded at least 445,000 times before its release, according to peer-to-peer monitoring firm BigChampagne.

Piracy grates on Bono [U2's lead singer], yet he's reluctant to lead a rebellion "because people think people like me are overpaid and overnourished, and they're not wrong," the U2 singer says. "What they're missing is, how does a songwriter get paid? There's no space for a Cole Porter [popular songwriter of the 1940s and 1950s] in the modern age.

"It's not the place for rich rock stars to ask for more money, but somebody should fight for fellow artists, because this is madness. Music has become tap water, a utility, where for me it's a sacred thing, so I'm a little offended."

The Internet has emasculated rather than liberated artists, he says, noting that the record industry has lost billions in value.

"From punk rock to hip-hop, from heavy metal to country, musicians walk along with a smile and jump like lemmings into the abyss," he says. "The music business has been thrown to the dogs legislatively."

That indifference will vanish once "file-sharing of TV shows and movies becomes as easy as songs," Bono says. "Somebody is going to call the cops."

—Edna Gundersen

And interactive websites have dramatically expanded public discourse. "Protections for intermediaries have been absolutely crucial for giving us the Internet today," said Fred von Lohmann, an EFF attorney.

A CHILLING LAW

Many Americans dislike the DMCA. The law's strongest opponents are scientists, librarians, academics, and free-speech advocates from all walks of life. These critics say that strict intellectual property protection in the electronic realm does society more harm than good. They say it jeopardizes privacy; limits fair use; and chills free expression, scientific research, and competition.

Lawrence Lessig is a law professor and a civil liberties activist. In his book *Free Culture*, he calls the DMCA a law "invoked to control the spread of information." Lessig and other DMCA critics believe the law destroys fair use and contradicts other cherished U.S. legal values.

Opponents explain that the DMCA, while not specifically outlawing fair use, renders various types of fair use impossible. The DMCA is supposed to support copyright law—but in practice, it actually changes the law. The DMCA

Above: Lawrence Lessig is a well-known critic of the DMCA. He believes it stifles fair use of copyrighted material.

puts citizens in a catch-22, or poses an unsolvable problem. For example, ElcomSoft's AEBP software enabled e-book buyers to use their e-books in several legal ways that publishers had prevented with electronic locks. Users had to pick these locks, which is illegal per DMCA, to exercise fair use, which is legal under general U.S. copyright law. Thus to exercise their legal rights with the AEBP, users had to break the law.

More disturbing to some, when someone stands accused of violating the DMCA by picking a digital lock, the question is not whether he or she violated a copyright. The question is whether the person used a technology that *could* violate a copyright. Simply having the

Fair Use

The following actions are examples of fair use of copyrighted material:

- Quoting an excerpt in a review or critique to illustrate a point or comment on the excerpt
- Quoting a short passage in a scholarly or technical work, for illustration or clarification of the author's own observations
- Reproducing some content of a work for use in a parody
- Summarizing a work, with brief quotations, in a news report
- Copying part of a work to repair a partially damaged library item
- Reproducing a small part of a work to illustrate a lesson or classroom project
- Copying a work in legislative or judicial proceedings or reports

Above: New technologies such as e-books pose a host of new questions about copyright law.

means to violate is enough to establish guilt.

Critics find this fact unacceptable because it defies the U.S. legal principle of presumed innocence. U.S. courts presume that people suspected of crimes are innocent unless and until they are proven guilty, but the DMCA declares them guilty simply for owning certain technology, such as the AEBP. To understand this law, think about a baseball bat. A baseball bat can serve not only its intended use as sporting equipment but also as a weapon. But U.S. society doesn't charge the owners of baseball bats with a crime just because their bats could be used improperly. If someone uses a baseball bat to hurt someone else, only then does society charge him or her with a crime—the crime of assault. But under the DMCA, just owning certain technology can get a person in trouble.

Some copyright owners have brought lawsuits under the DMCA's anti-circumvention provision. For example, in 2000 a media industry group called the Secure Digital Music Initiative (SDMI) publicly challenged digital technology experts to pick its electronic locks. A team of researchers from Princeton and Rice universities and Xerox Corporation took up the challenge—and succeeded. When the team tried to report its research results at an academic conference, SDMI threatened a DMCA lawsuit. It forced the researchers to withdraw their paper from the conference. They had to file a countersuit to publish a portion of their security research at a later conference. After this experience, at least one researcher chose to avoid further research in the field of electronic security. Thus the DMCA led in this case to the stifling of both academic freedom and free speech.

Also in response to the law, ISPs and websites have censored discussions of copy-protection systems because they worry that such discussions violate the DMCA ban on distributing lock-picking technology. The EFF predicts, "These developments will ultimately result in weakened security for all computer users (including, ironically, for copyright owners counting on technical measures to protect their works), as security researchers shy away from research that might run afoul of [the DMCA]."

Copyright owners have also used the DMCA's anti-circumvention provision to deter competition. For example, after companies created software that lets people play Sony's PlayStation console games on personal computers, Sony used the anti-circumvention provision to sue the companies. The companies had not engaged in piracy but had engaged

The World's Biggest Library

In 2004 the Internet search company Google began an ambitious project. It started to scan and digitize books to create a massive, searchable database. The database, called Google Books, allows Internet users to search within books. If a book is under copyright, the search results show just snippets of text or sample pages, plus information on how to buy or borrow the book. If the book is no longer under copyright, the searcher can download the book or read it online. Google began by scanning the collections of five major libraries. It plans to eventually scan every book ever published.

The project has faced legal challenges from associations of publishers and authors, who charge that it violates copyright law. In 2008 and 2009, Google settled with the authors and publishers, giving them a larger share of income from online advertising and book sales generated by the project. But many questions remain. What about online privacy? Do we really want Google tracking our reading habits? Will Americans feel free to read anything they want if they know the company might be watching? Google Books has set up a policy to protect readers' privacy, but the Electronic Freedom Foundation says it's not strict enough.

Other critics say that the 2008 and 2009 settlements give Google Books too much control over the distribution and pricing of digitized books. A group called the Open Book Alliance, which includes Microsoft, Amazon, and Yahoo, is fighting to open up the digitized book business to more competition.

in unlawful circumvention, Sony charged. Although developing interoperable software is fair use, the small companies could not bear the high cost of fighting Sony in court and pulled their products off the market. Thus the DMCA has become a new legal weapon that big companies can use to threaten small competitors.

Opponents of the DMCA find its notice-and-takedown provision equally problematic. They say it gives copyright owners "unwarranted leverage [unchecked power] over service providers and their subscribers."

Online intermediaries want to preserve their immunity from lawsuits. So when they receive notice of copyright infringement, they take down the material immediately, "without evaluating the claim for reasonableness or accuracy, or considering the fair use rights of users." But some takedown notices lack validity. For example, in 2007 magician Uri Geller sent a DMCA takedown notice to YouTube. Geller demanded takedown of a video that debunked his tricks. He didn't own copyright to the video or anything in it, but his notice got the video removed, at least until a lawsuit brought about its reposting.

That same year, the television and movie company Viacom sent more than one hundred thousand takedown notices based on a general search for its shows on YouTube. Viacom seeks millions—possibly billions—of dollars in damages from YouTube, claiming YouTube deliberately committed massive copyright infringement. This case was undecided at the end of 2009. But analysts say it threatens online intermediaries' immunity under the notice-and-takedown provision.

A NEW APPROACH

Americans disagree on the effects and the fairness of the DMCA. They do agree, however, that the law is imperfect.

To address the law's flaws, in 2003 and again in 2005, a group of U.S. representatives introduced a bill called the Digital Media Consumers' Rights Act (DMCRA). According to its authors, the DMCRA would have restored the balance in copyright law. Among other things, the DMCRA stated that picking a digital lock would not be a DMCA violation if the act did not violate the work's copyright. For example, an e-book owner could bypass electronic protections for the purpose of reading the e-book on a different device. However, if the owner were to upload the book onto the Internet

Most-used Internet services

Types of online content services used by U.S. adults in April, by percentage of respondents:

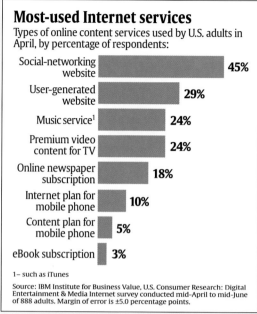

Social-networking website	45%
User-generated website	29%
Music service[1]	24%
Premium video content for TV	24%
Online newspaper subscription	18%
Internet plan for mobile phone	10%
Content plan for mobile phone	5%
eBook subscription	3%

1– such as iTunes

Source: IBM Institute for Business Value, U.S. Consumer Research: Digital Entertainment & Media Internet survey conducted mid-April to mid-June of 888 adults. Margin of error is ±5.0 percentage points.

By Marcy E. Mullins, USA TODAY, 2007

and share it with others, the act would be both a copyright and a DMCA violation. In addition, the DMCRA would have allowed scholars to research computer security without fear of breaking the law.

The DMCRA never became law. And by 2010, no one had revived it or introduced a similar bill. If the DMCA is such a problematic law, why haven't lawmakers fixed it? The answer to this question might lie in John Perry Barlow's essay:

> Intellectual property law cannot be patched, retrofitted, or expanded to contain digitized expression. . . . We will need to develop an entirely new set of methods as befits this entirely new set of circumstances.

In other words, Barlow believes the DMCA might be unfixable. He thinks it's time for an entirely new approach to intellectual property. But what shape that approach will take remains to be seen.

Epilogue

The Future of Online Freedom

MORE THAN TWO CENTURIES AFTER THE FOUNDING of the United States, the nation and its people have seen countless changes. But one thing has not changed: Americans continue to believe that freedom of speech is critical to democracy.

The United States has, nonetheless, struggled over how to apply the First Amendment's free speech protections to electronic media. As telephone, radio, film, television, and computers developed during the 1900s, policy makers at first resisted equating them with the printing press. Lawmakers and judges were reluctant to give these media First Amendment protection.

As the end of the century approached, the U.S. communications landscape changed dramatically. The Internet was born. It, in turn, spawned a wide and ever-growing array of tools that help people share information and ideas and do business with one another. Eventually, U.S. law recognized that electronic

Left: The technology involved with the Internet continues to evolve.

media are just as important to free expression as the printing press is.

WHERE DO WE STAND?

This recognition hasn't prevented efforts to restrict online communication, however. Some Americans believe that censoring online material is the best way to achieve or preserve important public goals. Meanwhile, other Americans strenuously oppose censorship, believing that it does more harm than good.

Some types of Internet censorship have been more successful than others. For example, bans on material inherently and indisputably harmful to children—such as child pornography and cyberbullying—have succeeded. Laws that decrease personal privacy in the name of national security have

Above: Questions about Internet censorship continue to crop up as technology allows for faster and more varied service.

withstood strong opposition. Efforts to limit access to and usage of digital intellectual property have partially succeeded.

However, efforts to legislate general public morality—by limiting or banning online obscenity, adult pornography, defamation, bigotry, and fighting words—have failed. To protect computer security and prevent financial losses, the United States has a federal law restricting spam. But spammers ignore this law, so it too is a failure.

At the beginning of the twenty-first century, evidence shows that Americans are fairly evenly split over the need for Internet censorship. U.S. laws, court decisions, and public opinion polls reveal a mixed public response to various censorship attempts.

In a 2007 U.S. poll by tech research firms Zogby International and 463 Communications, 53 percent of respondents said the government should exercise some control over Internet content such as video. In a 2008 University of Connecticut poll, 54 percent of respondents said they would favor a government proposal to provide free nationwide Internet access equipped with filters to block indecent or obscene material.

Public attitudes on security-related censorship show a similar split. In 2006 the ACLU published a poll of more than one thousand registered voters across the political spectrum. It found that 55

> "There is a rapidly expanding trend for the Internet to be used by governments and companies to exert control over what individuals can and cannot say, and the ways in which they can use the Internet."
>
> —NICK DEARDEN, CAMPAIGN MANAGER FOR HUMAN RIGHTS GROUP AMNESTY INTERNATIONAL, 2008

percent of respondents believed warrantless wiretapping is illegal and wanted Congress to demand a halt to the practice. In the same poll, 66 percent wanted changes made to the PATRIOT Act. A 2009 *USA TODAY*–Gallup poll found that 63 percent of Americans favored investigation into whether Bush administration policies, including warrantless wiretapping and the PATRIOT Act, violated the law.

Public opinion on electronic intellectual property issues is harder to analyze. Between 1998 and 2009, no major organizations published opinion polls on copyright laws such as the DMCA.

WHERE ARE WE HEADED?

In 2008 Elon University and the Pew Internet and American Life Project conducted a survey called "The Future of the Internet III." About twelve hundred leading Internet builders, activists, and analysts gave their opinions about the effect of the Internet on social, political, and economic life in the year 2020.

The Elon–Pew survey did not specifically target censorship issues, but it did produce some relevant predictions:

- Respondents nearly all agreed that the concept of privacy is changing and that privacy itself is decreasing. They split equally in their views on whether this scenario would be good or bad for society.
- About 56 percent of participants did not think the Internet would do much to promote social tolerance. They believed electronic communications would actually "expand the potential for hate, bigotry, and terrorism." They explained that the human tendency "to congregate with like-minded allies and act in tribes is too potent to be overcome by technology tools."
- About 60 percent of respondents believed that legislatures, courts, and industry would not be able to control intellectual property use. They said "'cracking' technology will

stay ahead of technology to control intellectual property (IP) or policy regulating IP."

- Survey participants (80 percent) agreed overwhelmingly that the existing structure of the Internet will endure. Many also believed there would be "more separated Internet spaces, created by governments and corporations to maintain network control." That is, organizations will create subnetworks on the Internet. These subnetworks will each have their own rules about permissible content.

Microsoft cofounder Bill Gates has made many predictions about computers and society. Though his record isn't perfect, several of his predictions have come true.

Above: As cofounder of Microsoft, Bill Gates has spent most of his adult life heavily involved with the evolution of computers and the Internet.

" You cannot control the Internet. "

—BILL GATES, MICROSOFT COFOUNDER, 2008

Gates is optimistic about the future of online freedom. He believes that efforts to restrict the exchange of information on the Internet will always fail in the end. "You cannot control the Internet," he insisted in a speech at California's Stanford University. He went on to explain that limiting free speech curbs commercial activity, so businesses tend to fight censorship. "If your country wants to have a developed economy... you basically have to open up the Internet."

What is fair? How can the United States protect the free

Above: The Internet is becoming a vital part of daily life in the United States. And with increased importance of the Internet comes a louder debate about freedom and censorship in cyberspace.

speech rights of all without putting some people in harm's way? How can policy makers protect children, provide security, and promote innovation without trampling democracy? How should Internet laws ensure the greatest possible benefit to U.S. society?

No easy answers exist. A tightly controlled Internet is unrealistic, while an uncontrolled Internet could be dangerous. The Internet is still young, and its ever-changing character complicates matters. There's only one sure thing about Internet censorship: the debate is just getting started.

TIMELINE

1776 The Second Continental Congress approves the Declaration of Independence, giving birth to the United States of America.

1787 U.S. leaders adopt the Constitution.

1791 U.S. lawmakers adopt the Bill of Rights.

1798 Congress passes the Alien and Sedition Acts, banning speech critical of the U.S. government.

1861–1865 President Abraham Lincoln shuts down newspapers that threatened the federal government's efforts in the Civil War.

1873 Anthony Comstock founds the New York Society for the Suppression of Vice. Congress passes the Comstock Act.

1878 Bostonians found the Watch and Ward Society.

1917 Congress passes the Espionage Act, broadly expanding the U.S. legal meaning of *espionage*. The National Civil Liberties Bureau (NCLB) forms to provide legal aid to people arrested under the act.

1918 Congress strengthens the Espionage Act by passing the Sedition Act.

1919 Three Supreme Court decisions—*Schenck v. United States*, *Debs v. United States*, and *Abrams v. United States*—uphold the Sedition Act.

1920 The NCLB changes its name to the American Civil Liberties Union (ACLU).

1921 Congress repeals the Espionage Act and the Sedition Act. U.S. courts declare James Joyce's novel *Ulysses* to be obscene and ban it from the United States.

1925   The Supreme Court decision *Gitlow v. New York* rules that the First Amendment applies not only to the federal government but also to the states.

1931   In *Stromberg v. California*, the high court rules that the First Amendment can protect nonverbal "speech." *Near v. Minnesota* strikes down the Minnesota Gag Law.

1933   A federal court rules that *Ulysses* is neither obscene nor illegal, opening the door to U.S. publication of serious literature with coarse language or sexual subject matter.

1938   The *Life* magazine article "Birth of a Baby" is banned as obscene. A New York court rules in favor of *Life*, opening the door to other publications on reproductive issues.

1940   Congress passes the Smith Act, making it illegal to advocate overthrowing the U.S. government by force or violence.

1942   The Supreme Court decision *Chaplinsky v. New Hampshire* rules that the First Amendment does not protect fighting words.

1949   The Federal Communications Commission enacts the fairness doctrine, which requires radio and television broadcasters to present controversial issues in a balanced way.

1952   In *Burstyn v. Wilson*, the high court finds that free speech protections apply to motion pictures.

1957   In *Butler v. Michigan*, the Supreme Court strikes down a Michigan law outlawing printed matter with obscene language.

1968   The ruling in *Ginsberg v. New York* says that state laws can create stricter obscenity standards for children than for adults.

1969   *Stanley v. Georgia* establishes that states cannot punish private possession of obscene material.

1973 *Miller v. California* establishes a definition of the term *obscenity* and gives states greater power to censor obscene material.

1978 The National Socialist Party of America (NSPA) wins the right to demonstrate in a largely Jewish suburb of Chicago.

1982 The U.S. Supreme Court rules in *New York v. Ferber* that the First Amendment does not protect child pornography.

1987 The U.S. Supreme Court rules that the fairness doctrine need not be enforced. President Ronald Reagan vetoes a new law establishing a fairness doctrine.

1988 In *Hustler Magazine Inc. v. Falwell*, the Supreme Court upholds the right of the press to parody public figures.

1989 The World Wide Web is invented.

1996 Congress passes the Child Pornography Prevention Act (CPPA) and the Communications Decency Act (CDA) to regulate Internet pornography.

1997 The Supreme Court strikes down the CDA in *Reno v. ACLU*.

1998 Congress passes the Child Online Protection Act (COPA) to replace the CDA. Congress passes the Digital Millennium Copyright Act (DMCA) to prevent the illegal copying of electronic works. Brandon Beussink builds a website critical of his school, leading to a court battle that Beussink wins.

1999 The file-sharing service Napster launches.

2000 Congress passes the Children's Internet Protection Act (CIPA), requiring libraries and schools to place pornography filters on computers. The Children's Online Privacy Protection Act (COPPA) requires parental consent for collecting or using the personal information of Internet users under thirteen years old.

2001   Congress passes the PATRIOT Act, giving law enforcement agencies more power to search telephone, e-mail, and other records. President George Bush authorizes the President's Surveillance Program (PSP), or warrantless wiretapping. Russian programmer Dmitry Sklyarov is arrested and detained for violating the DMCA.

2003   A federal court finds COPA unconstitutional. President Bush signs the CAN-SPAM Act to regulate spam. Congress passes the Protect Act to criminalize the creation and distribution of child pornography.

2005   A group of U.S. representatives introduces the Digital Media Consumers' Rights Act (DMCRA) to balance DMCA.

2006   Congress renews the PATRIOT Act.

2008   Congress reauthorizes warrantless wiretapping. Google Books reaches a settlement with publishers and authors regarding digitized books and copyright infringement.

2009   Federal lawmakers introduce the Megan Meier Cyberbullying Prevention Act (H.R. 1966) and the Internet Stopping Adults Facilitating the Exploitation of Today's Youth (Internet Safety) Act. A group of U.S. senators introduces the Judicious Use of Surveillance Tools in Counter-terrorism Efforts (JUSTICE) Act to replace the PATRIOT Act.

GLOSSARY

bigotry: hatred or intolerance of a particular group of people

censorship: forbidding, silencing, or punishing undesirable speech

checks and balances: the ability of each branch of government to limit the acts of other branches

civil liberty: freedom from government interference

Constitution: a document adopted in 1787 that defines the basic principles and laws of the United States

copyright: the exclusive right to reproduce, publish, and sell a literary, musical, or artistic work

cyberbullying: harassing a child electronically, such as through the Internet or by cell phone

defamation: lying to harm others

democracy: government by the people through free elections

espionage: spying; passing secret information to an enemy

fair use: the legal use of copyrighted materials

fighting words: speech intended to provoke violence

First Amendment: a 1791 addition to the U.S. Constitution that guarantees Americans freedom of speech, among other things

freedom of speech: the right to speak, write, and publish almost anything without fear of punishment

injunction: a court order requiring or forbidding a certain act

intellectual property: original works by authors, artists, and inventors

morality: principles or rules of good conduct

national security: efforts to protect a nation

national security letter: a written legal command requiring a business or organization to produce client records in strict secrecy and without judicial review

obscenity: speech that offends common sexual morals; content that many people find vulgar, raunchy, or disgusting

piracy: reproducing copyrighted material without the owner's permission

pornography: words or images that depict sexual behavior and intend to sexually excite the reader or viewer

prostitution: engaging in sexual relations for money

sedition: stirring up rebellion against authority

terrorist: someone who uses violence to create fear, usually to promote a movement or cause

warrantless wiretapping: secret monitoring of electronic communications originating outside the United States, to or from anyone suspected of terrorist links

SOURCE NOTES

5 Steve Pokin, "A Real Person, A Real Death," *St. Charles Journal*, November 10, 2007, http://stcharlesjournal.stltoday.com/articles/2007/11/10/news/ sj2tn20071110-1111stc_pokin_1.ii1.txt (October 28, 2009).

6 Ibid.

6 William M. Welch, "Woman Indicted in 'Cyberbullying' Case," USA TODAY, May 16, 2008, A3.

6–7 Christopher Maag, "A Hoax Turned Fatal Draws Anger but No Charges," New York Times, November 28, 2007, http://www.nytimes.com/2007/ 11/28/us/28hoax.html (November 28, 2009).

7–8 Linda Sanchez, "Text of H.R. 1966: Megan Meier Cyberbullying Prevention Act," Govtrack.us, April 2, 2009, http://www.govtrack.us/congress/ billtext.xpd?bill=h111-1966 (October 29, 2009).

8 Linda Sanchez, "Protecting Victims, Preserving Freedoms," Huffington Post, May 6, 2009, http://www.huffingtonpost.com/rep-linda-sanchez/ protecting-victims-preser_b_198079.html (October 29, 2009).

8 Lance Whitney, "Cyberbullying Case to Test Megan's Law," CNET News, August 28, 2009, http://news.cnet.com/8301-13578_3-10320274-38 .html (October 30, 2009).

8–9 Ibid.

9 Timothy Birdnow, "Cyberbullying Laws and the Moral Code," American Thinker, May 24, 2009, http://www.americanthinker.com/2009/05/ cyberbullying_laws_and_the_mor.html (October 30, 2009).

9 Whitney, "Cyberbullying Case."

9 Jacqui Cheng, "Trolling Someone Online? Bill Would Slap You with Jail Time," Ars Technica, May 10, 2009, http://arstechnica.com/tech-policy/ news/2009/05/trolling-someone-online-bill-would-slap-you-with-jail -time.ars (October 30, 2009).

9 Birdnow, "Cyberbullying."

12 Cheng, "Trolling."

15 Joint Committee on Printing, "The Constitution of the United States with Index and the Declaration of Independence," U.S. Government Printing Office, July 5, 2007, http://frwebgate.access.gpo.gov/cgi-bin/getdoc. cgi?dbname=110_cong_documents&docid=f:hd051.110.pdf (October 16, 2009).

17 Ibid.

17 Carl Cohen, "Free Speech and Political Extremism: How Nasty Are We Free to Be?" Law and Philosophy 7 (1989): 263–279.

20   Tom Long, "Dwight Long, Watch and Ward Society Leader, Dies," Boston Globe, January 1, 2005.

24   Oliver Wendell Holmes, "Opinion of the Court: Schenck v. United States," Cornell University Law School Legal Information Institute: Supreme Court Collection, March 3, 1919, http://supct.law.cornell.edu/supct/html/historics/USSC_CR_0249_0047_ZO.html (June 20, 2009).

24   Oliver Wendell Holmes, "Dissenting Opinion: Abrams v. United States," Cornell University Law School Legal Information Institute: Supreme Court Collection, November 10, 1919, http://supct.law.cornell.edu/supct/html/historics/USSC_CR_0250_0616_ZD.html (June 20, 2009).

24   Holmes, "Opinion of the Court: Schenck v. United States."

25   Holmes, "Dissenting Opinion: Abrams v. United States."

27   Joint Committee on Printing, "Constitution of the United States."

28–29   Charles Evans Hughes, "Opinion of the Court: Near v. Minnesota," Cornell University Law School Legal Information Institute: Supreme Court Collection, June 1, 1931, http://supct.law.cornell.edu/supct/html/historics/USSC_CR_0283_0697_ZO.html (October 21, 2009).

29   William Blackstone, "Blackstone's Commentaries on the Laws of England, Book Four, Chapter Eleven: Of Offenses Against the Public Peace," The Avalon Project, 2008, http://avalon.law.yale.edu/18th_century/blackstone_bk4ch11.asp (October 21, 2009).

31   Joel Silverman, "When Birth Was Obscene: Court Case Puts Pregnancy Back on Newsstands," National Sexuality Resource Center, January 10, 2004, http://nsrc.sfsu.edu/article/when_birth_was_obscene_court_case_puts_pregnancy_back_newsstands (October 22, 2009).

31   Ibid.

32   Frank Murphy, "Opinion of the Court: Chaplinsky v. New Hampshire," Cornell University Law School Legal Information Institute: Supreme Court Collection, March 9, 1942, http://www4.law.cornell.edu/supct/html/historics/USSC_CR_0315_0568_ZO.html (October 23, 2009).

33   Ibid.

33   Murphy, "Opinion of the Court: Chaplinsky v. New Hampshire."

34   William O. Douglas, "Opinion of the Court: Terminiello v. City of Chicago," FindLaw, May 16, 1949, http://laws.findlaw.com/us/337/1.html (October 23, 2009).

35   Felix Frankfurter, "Opinion of the Court: Butler v. State of Michigan," FindLaw, February 25, 1957, http://laws.findlaw.com/us/352/380.html (October 23, 2009).

35   William Brennan, "Opinion of the Court: Ginsberg v. New York," FindLaw, April 22, 1968, http://laws.findlaw.com/us/390/629.html (October 23, 2009).

35–36   Warren Burger, "Opinion of the Court: Miller v. California," Cornell University Law School Legal Information Institute: Supreme Court Collection, June 21, 1973, http://www.law.cornell.edu/supct/html/historics/USSC_CR_0413_0015_ZO.html (October 25, 2009).

41   Supreme Court of the United States, "Syllabus: Hustler Magazine, Inc. v. Falwell," Cornell University Law School Legal Information Institute: Supreme Court Collection, February 24, 1988, http://www.law.cornell.edu/supct/html/historics/USSC_CR_0485_0046_ZS.html (November 24, 2009).

44   Robert Jackson, "Concurring Opinion: Kovacs v. Cooper," FindLaw, January 31, 1949, http://laws.findlaw.com/us/336/77.html (November 11, 2009).

44   Byron White, "Opinion of the Court: Red Lion Broadcasting Co. v. FCC," FindLaw, June 9, 1969, http://laws.findlaw.com/us/395/367.html (November 11, 2009).

46   104th Congress of the United States of America, "Telecommunications Act of 1996: Title V—Obscenity and Violence," U.S. Government Printing Office, January 3, 1996, http://frwebgate.access.gpo.gov/cgi-bin/getdoc.cgi?dbname=104_cong_bills&docid=f:s652enr.txt.pdf (November 13, 2009).

47   John Paul Stevens, "Opinion of the Court: Reno v. American Civil Liberties Union," Cornell University Law School Legal Information Institute: Supreme Court Collection, June 26, 1997, http://www4.law.cornell.edu/supct/html/historics/USSC_CR_0521_0844_ZO.html (November 13, 2009).

50   Stewart Dalzell, "American Civil Liberties Union, et al., v. Janet Reno," MIT Student Association for Freedom of Expression, June 11, 1996, http://www.mit.edu/activities/safe/legal/cda-decision.html (November 16, 2009).

50   106th Congress of the United States of America, "Child Online Protection Act," COPA Commission, October 23, 1998, http://www.copacommission.org/commission/original.shtml (November 13, 2009).

57   Jay Sekulow, "Kids Need Law's Protection," USA TODAY, June 30, 2004, A12.

62   Anne Collier, "Internet Safety News: Amy's Story," NetSmartz Workshop, n.d., http://www.netsmartz.org/news/amystory.htm (August 17, 2009).

63 Nielsen Company, "Growing Up, and Growing Fast: Kids 2-11 Spending More Time Online," nielsen wire, July 6, 2009, http://blog.nielsen.com/nielsenwire/online_mobile/growing-up-and-growing-fast-kids-2-11-spending-more-time-online/ (August 18, 2009).

68 Chip Pickering, "Freedoms Are Not at Risk," *USA TODAY*, March 5, 2003, A12.

69 Marc Rotenberg, "EPIC Board and Staff," Electronic Privacy Information *Center*, n.d., http://epic.org/epic/staff/rotenberg/ (September 4, 2009).

69 Alberto R. Gonzalez, "Target Sexual Predators," *USA TODAY*, May 14, 2008, A11.

71 Tony Mauro, "Taming the Internet Court's Task to Protect Kids But Not Censor," *USA TODAY*, March 18, 1997, A1.

72 Deirdre Donahue, "Stop Fretting: This Is the 'Best Time' to Be a Kid," *USA TODAY*, October 1, 1998, D2.

75 Stephen C. Balkam, Kimberly A. Scardino, and Jennifer A. Hanley, "Comments of the Family Online Safety Institute before the Federal Communications Commission," Family Online Safety Institute, April 16, 2009, http://www.fosi.org/cms/images/stories/news_pdfs/fosifccnoifiledcomments.pdf (September 11, 2009).

77–78 Declan Mccullagh, "School Dazed by Speech Ruling," *Wired*, December 29, 1998, http://www.wired.com/politics/law/news/1998/12/17068 (September 8, 2009).

78 Ibid.

78 Rodney W. Sippel, "Beussink v. Woodland R-IV School," Hofstra University Faculty Homepage: Peter J. Spiro, December 28, 1998, http://people.hofstra.edu/peter_j_spiro/beussink.htm (September 11, 2009).

78 Mccullagh, "School Dazed."

79 New England Survey Research Associates, "State of the First Amendment 2008," First Amendment Center, September 17, 2008, http://www.firstamendmentcenter.org/pdf/SOFA2008survey.pdf (September 11, 2009).

81 Christopher Wolf, "Racists, Bigots, and the Law on the Internet," Anti-Defamation League, July 2000, http://www.adl.org/internet/internet_law3.asp (September 11, 2009).

82 Karen Thomas and Elizabeth Weise, "Hate Groups Snare Youths with Web Games," *USA TODAY*, July 8, 1999.

83 Marisol Bello, "White Supremacists' New Angle," *USA TODAY*, October 21, 2008, A3.

85   CP80 Foundation, "Like Putting Gasoline on Fire: The Proliferation of Internet Pornography and Its Effect on Human Sex Trafficking," CP80, 2007, http://www.cp80.org/resources/0000/0066/CP80_Foundation_-_Internet_Pornography_and_Human_Sex_Trafficking.pdf (November 25, 2009).

88   Joan Biskupic, "It May Be Up to Parents to Block Web Porn; In Rejecting Online Law, Court Suggests Using Computer Filters," *USA TODAY*, June 30, 2004, A6.

88   Ibid.

89   Sippel, "Beussink v. Woodland R-IV School."

93   *USA TODAY* editors, "Election-Year Spying Deal Is Flawed, Overly Broad," *USA TODAY*, June 25, 2008, A8.

95   Richard Willing, "With Only a Letter, FBI Can Gather Private Data; National Security Letters' reach expanded after 9/11," *USA TODAY*, July 6, 2006, A1.

96   Ibid.

96   *USA TODAY* editors, "Bush Uses Scare Tactics to Railroad Flawed Spying Act," *USA TODAY*, February 14, 2008, A12.

96   Peter Eisler, "Senate OKs Surveillance Revamp," *USA TODAY*, July 10, 2008, A7.

96   Kit Bond, "Track Terror Threats," *USA TODAY*, June 25, 2008, A8.

96   Ibid.

96   Benjamin Franklin, *Memoirs of the Life and Writings of Benjamin Franklin, LL.D.,* ed. William Temple Franklin (London: Henry Colburn, 1818).

100   Willing, "With Only a Letter."

100   Ibid.

103   Russell Feingold, "Statements on Introduced Bills and Joint Resolutions," Govtrack.us, September 17, 2009, http://www.govtrack.us/congress/record.xpd?id=111-s20090917-46 (September 23, 2009).

108   Stephen Tully, *International Documents on Corporate Responsibility* (Northampton, MA: Edward Elgar Publishing, 2007), ii.

109   Lawrence Lessig, *Code: Version 2.0* (New York: Basic Books, 2006), 182.

110–111   John Perry Barlow, "The Economy of Ideas," *Wired*, March 1994, http://www.wired.com/wired/archive/2.03/economy.ideas.html (October 6, 2009).

111   Ibid.

121   David Kravets, "10 Years Later, Misunderstood DMCA Is the Law That Saved the Web," *Wired*, October 27, 2008, http://www.wired.com/threatlevel/2008/10/ten-years-later/ (October 13, 2009).

121   Lawrence Lessig, *Free Culture: How Big Media Uses Technology and the Law to Lock Down Culture and Control Creativity* (New York: Penguin Press, 2004), 157.

124   Electronic Frontier Foundation, "Unintended Consequences: Ten Years under the DMCA," Electronic Frontier Foundation, October 2008, http://www.eff.org/wp/unintended-consequences-ten-years-under-dmca (October 14, 2009).

125–126   Kevin O'Keefe and Wendy Seltzer, "Regional Overviews: United States and Canada," OpenNet Initiative, 2007, http://opennet.net/research/regions/namerica (October 14, 2009).

126   Kravets, "10 Years Later."

127   Barlow, "Economy of Ideas."

131   Janna Quitney Anderson and Lee Rainie, "The Future of the Internet III," Imagining the Internet, December 14, 2008, http://www.elon.edu/docs/e-web/predictions/2008_survey.pdf (November 19, 2009).

132   Ibid.

132   Ibid.

133   Ibid.

133   Ibid.

134   Ibid.

134   Robert McMillan, "Internet Censorship Won't Work," *Computer World*, February 20, 2008, http://www.computerworld.com/s/article/print/9063598/Bill_Gates_says_Internet_censorship_won_t_work?taxonomyName=Internet&taxonomyId=167 (November 28, 2009).

SELECTED BIBLIOGRAPHY

Baase, Sara. *A Gift of Fire: Social, Legal, and Ethical Issues for Computing and the Internet.* Upper Saddle River, NJ: Pearson Education, 2008.

Barlow, John Perry. "The Economy of Ideas." *Wired.* March 1994. http://www.wired.com/wired/archive/2.03/economy.ideas.html (November 5, 2009).

Bidgoli, Hossein. *The Internet Encyclopedia.* Vol. 2. Hoboken, NJ: John Wiley and Sons, 2004.

Condé Nast Digital. "Blogs." *Wired.* 2009. http://www.wired.com/blogs (November 4, 2009).

——. "Politics." *Wired.* 2009. http://www.wired.com/politics (November 4, 2009).

Cornell University Law School. "Supreme Court Collection." Legal Information Institute. 2009. http://supct.law.cornell.edu/supct/index.html (November 4, 2009).

Deibert, Ronald, John Palfrey, Rafal Rohozinski, and Jonathan Zittrain. *Access Denied: The Practice and Policy of Global Internet Filtering.* Cambridge, MA: MIT Press, 2008.

Electronic Frontier Foundation. "Unintended Consequences: Ten Years under the DMCA." Electronic Frontier Foundation. October 2008. http://www.eff.org/wp/unintended-consequences-ten-years-under-dmca (October 14, 2009).

First Amendment Center. "First Amendment Topics." First Amendment Center. 2009. http://www.firstamendmentcenter.org/topicssummary.aspx (November 4, 2009).

Joint Committee on Printing. "The Constitution of the United States with Index and the Declaration of Independence." U.S. Government Printing Office. July 5, 2007. http://frwebgate.access.gpo.gov/cgi-bin/getdoc.cgi?dbname=110_cong_documents&docid=f:hd051.110.pdf (October 16, 2009).

Lessig, Lawrence. *Code: Version 2.0.* New York: Basic Books, 2006.

————. *Free Culture: How Big Media Uses Technology and the Law to Lock Down Culture and Control Creativity.* New York: Penguin Press, 2004.

National Center for Missing and Exploited Children. "Statistics." NetSmartz Workshop. 2006. http://www.netsmartz.org/safety/statistics.htm (November 5, 2009).

National Coalition Against Censorship. "A Selective Timeline of the Internet and Censorship." National Coalition Against Censorship. March 10, 2009. http://www.ncac.org/internet/Timeline (November 5, 2009).

O'Keefe, Kevin, and Wendy Seltzer. "Regional Overviews: United States and Canada." OpenNet Initiative. 2007. http://opennet.net/research/regions/namerica (October 14, 2009).

Pew Research Center. "Data Tools." Pew Internet and American Life Project. 2009. http://www.pewinternet.org/Data-Tools.aspx (November 4, 2009).

————. "Explore Our Topics." Pew Internet and American Life Project. 2009. http://www.pewinternet.org/Topics.aspx (November 4, 2009).

Russomanno, Joseph. *Defending the First: Commentary on First Amendment Issues and Cases.* Mahwah, NJ: Lawrence Erlbaum Associates, 2005.

Schwabach, Aaron. *Internet and the Law: Technology, Society, and Compromises.* Santa Barbara, CA: ABC-CLIO, 2006.

US Legal. "United States Censorship." US Legal Lawdigest. 2004. http://lawdigest.uslegal.com/first-amendment-law/censorship/7240/ (November 5, 2009).

Wolf, Christopher. "Racists, Bigots and the Law on the Internet." Anti-Defamation League. July 2000. http://www.adl.org/internet/internet_law3.asp (November 4, 2009).

ORGANIZATIONS TO CONTACT

American Civil Liberties Union

125 Broad Street, 18th Floor
New York, NY 10004
212-549-2666
http://www.aclu.org
The ACLU is a nonprofit group that works in U.S. courts, legislatures, and communities to defend and preserve the individual rights and liberties guaranteed by the Constitution and other U.S. laws. These rights include First Amendment rights, protection against illegal discrimination, and privacy.

American Library Association (ALA)

50 East Huron
Chicago, IL 60611
800-545-2433
http://www.ala.org
The ALA is a national organization of library professionals committed to diversity, education, intellectual freedom, and literacy. ALA is a vocal opponent of censorship efforts aimed at U.S. libraries.

CP80 Foundation

1507 North Technology Way, Suite 1300
Orem, UT 84097
801-705-4242
http://www.cp80.org
CP80 is a nonprofit group that advocates regulating the Internet to make it easier for users to filter out pornography. The foundation supports using education, Internet governance, and legislation to achieve its goals.

Electronic Freedom Foundation (EFF)

454 Shotwell Street
San Francisco, CA 94110-1914
415-436-9333
http://www.eff.org
The EFF is a legal advocacy organization. It defends digital free speech,

privacy, innovation, and consumer rights by providing free legal aid.
The group also advises lawmakers and educates the press and public.

Family Research Council (FRC)
801 G Street, NW
Washington, DC 20001
202-393-2100
http://www.frc.org
The FRC promotes traditional Judeo-Christian family values and ethics
in national policy. It supports vigorous enforcement of existing laws
and the enactment of new laws against the distribution of obscene
materials.

Internet Education Foundation (IEF)
1634 I Street NW, Suite 1100
Washington, DC 20006
202-638-4370
http://www.neted.org
The IEF is an Internet industry group dedicated to teaching the
public and policy makers how a free and global Internet can promote
communication, commerce, and democracy. The IEF operates
GetNetWise (http://www.getnetwise.org), a user-friendly resource
intended to help ordinary people make informed decisions about their
Internet use. It offers information on children's online safety, unwanted
e-mail and spam, Internet security, and privacy.

Morality in Media (MIM)
475 Riverside Drive, Suite 239
New York, NY 10115
212-870-3222
http://www.moralityinmedia.org
MIM is a national nonprofit organization that combats obscenity and
upholds decency standards in the media. Its motto is "Promoting a
Decent Society Through Law." MIM maintains the National Obscenity
Law Center (http://www.moralityinmedia.org/nolc/index.htm), a
clearinghouse of legal materials on obscenity law. It also conducts
programs to educate and involve concerned citizens.

National Center for Missing and Exploited Children (NCMEC)

Charles B. Wang International Children's Building
699 Prince Street
Alexandria, VA 22314-3175
703-224-2150
http://www.missingkids.com

The NCMEC's mission is to help prevent child abduction and sexual exploitation, to help find missing children, and to assist victims of child abduction and sexual exploitation, their families, and the professionals who serve them. NCMEC operates the NetSmartz Workshop (http://www.netsmartz.org), an interactive, educational resource for children, parents, guardians, educators, and law enforcement. The workshop uses age-appropriate activities to teach children how to stay safe on the Internet.

National Coalition Against Censorship (NCAC)

275 Seventh Avenue, Suite 1504
New York, NY 10001
212-807-6222
http://www.ncac.org

The NCAC is an alliance of fifty literary, artistic, religious, educational, professional, labor, and civil liberties groups. These groups share the belief that freedom of thought, inquiry, and expression is a fundamental human right and is essential to a healthy democracy. The NCAC works to educate its members and the public about the dangers of censorship and how to oppose them.

Recording Industry Association of America (RIAA)

1025 F Street NW, Tenth Floor
Washington, DC 20004
202-775-0101
http://www.riaa.com

The RIAA is the trade group that represents the U.S. recording industry. It promotes a legal climate that supports creativity and financial vitality in the music business. The RIAA works to protect intellectual property rights worldwide.

FURTHER INFORMATION

BOOKS

Axelrod-Contrada, Joan. *Reno v. ACLU: Internet Censorship.* Tarrytown, NY: Marshall Cavendish Benchmark, 2006.
In this volume, the author discusses the landmark case that overturned the Communications Decency Act of 1996, which tried to limit online content for people under eighteen years of age.

Herumin, Wendy. *Censorship on the Internet: From Filters to Freedom of Speech.* Berkeley Heights, NJ: Enslow, 2004.
This book examines efforts to control Internet content and access in order to protect children from harmful material. It also discusses resistance to these efforts by free-speech advocates.

Menhard, Francha Roffé. *Internet Issues: Pirates, Censors, and Cybersquatters.* Berkeley Heights, NJ: Enslow, 2001.
This book examines some of the major issues raised by the Internet explosion of the early twenty-first century. These issues include filtering, privacy, piracy, security, scams, hate groups, predators, and pornography.

Nakaya, Andrea C. *Censorship: Opposing Viewpoints.* Farmington Hills, MI: Greenhaven, 2005.
The authors in this anthology of essays explore censorship on the Internet, censorship in relation to the U.S. war on terrorism, whether free speech should be censored, and whether censorship threatens freedom in the United States.

FILMS

Good Morning, Vietnam. DVD. Burbank, CA: Walt Disney Video, 1998.
This film begins in 1965, during the Vietnam War (1957–1975). It's based on the real-life experiences of air force sergeant Adrian Cronauer. Cronauer, a disc jockey, works for Armed Forces Radio in Saigon, Vietnam. Cronauer sharply contrasts with the dull deejays before him. He starts each broadcast yelling, "Goooooood morning, Vietnaaaaam!" He plays banned rock-and-roll music. He rattles off

irreverent comedy monologues and pokes fun at everyone. Cronauer's superior tries to take his job away, but Cronauer's popularity with the top brass protects him. After personally experiencing the horrors of war, he insists on telling the truth instead of the government-censored version of the news—even though he knows the military will punish him for it.

WEBSITES

Debatepedia

http://wiki.idebate.org
This website is a project of the International Debate Education Association. Its purpose is to clarify public debates and improve decision making. It uses the same collaborative technology that powers Wikipedia. People across the nation and around the world can join one another in more than twelve hundred debates on important public issues. Debatepedia includes dozens of active debates on questions related to the Internet and freedom of speech, such as:

• Is it ever right for governments to restrict freedom of speech?
• Should denial of the Holocaust be illegal?
• Should the government censor the violent or expletive-filled song lyrics?
• Should intellectual property rights be abolished
• Is it acceptable to sacrifice some individual liberties in the interest of national security?
• Should unregulated distribution of copyrighted works over Internet be allowed?

First Amendment Center

http://www.firstamendmentcenter.org
The First Amendment Center at Vanderbilt University in Nashville, Tennessee, operates this website. It features thorough research on key First Amendment issues and topics, daily First Amendment news, a First Amendment library, and guest analyses by respected legal specialists.

Peacefire

http://www.peacefire.org

Peacefire is a website dedicated to preserving First Amendment rights for Internet users—especially minors, people whose employers censor the Internet, people serving in the military, and people living in countries that have filtering systems. Bennett Haselton, a teenager at the time, started Peacefire in 1996 to educate young people about the Communications Decency Act. Since then the site has grown to include lists of websites blocked by popular Internet filters and instructions for disabling filters.

War Feels Like War

http://www.pbs.org/pov/warfeelslikewar

The Iraq war, which began in 2003, introduced "embedded" reporters to the world. Embedded reporters must follow strict rules created by the U.S. military. Embedding lets the military better control which information reaches Americans at home. *War Feels Like War*, a public television documentary, is the story of an international group of journalists who refused to be embedded. These reporters ventured onto the battlefield without military protection and frequently without guides. They often found themselves reporting the stories that went untold by their embedded colleagues: civilian deaths, injuries, chaos in the streets, and mixed receptions for soldiers. This website offers a movie trailer and broadcast schedule, as well as a wealth of additional resources for exploring the topic of news censorship.

INDEX

abortion, 48–49

Advanced e-Book Processor (AEBP), 105–106, 122

Alien and Sedition Acts, 18

American Civil Liberties Union (ACLU), 11, 26, 29, 49, 102, 131

antiobscenity law, 19–20

artists, payment of, 112–113, 120

banned books, 20, 21, 29–31, 46–47

Barlow, John Perry, 110–112, 127

Beeson, Ann, 100

Beussink, Brandon, 77–78, 81, 89

Bill of Rights, 16–17

Birdnow, Timothy, 10

"Birth of a Baby," 30–31

Black, Don, 82–83

Blackstone, William, 29

Bond, Kit, 96

books: censored, 20, 21, 29–31, 46–47; digital, 105, 122, 125

Boston, MA, 20, 22

Burger, Warren, 35–36

Bush, George W., 69, 96, 102

CAN-SPAM Act, 58–59

censorship, 12, 17–18; child safety and, 12, 67–69; history of, 15–41; Internet and, 12, 43–59, 101, 130–132, 134–135; privacy and, 92–93; wartime, 24–25, 33

Chaplinsky, Walter, 32–33

chat rooms, online, 66, 74

checks and balances, 97

Child Online Protection Act (COPA), 50, 51, 54–55, 56–57

child pornography, 37, 88

Child Pornography Prevention Act (CPPA), 46

Children's Internet Protection Act (CIPA), 52, 67

child safety, 12, 34, 35, 37; Internet and, 45–47, 50, 54–57, 63–75, 88, 135; parents role in, 69–75

child safety laws: 46, 50, 51, 52, 54–55, 56–57, 67

China, 101

civility, 13

Civil War, 18–19

clear and present danger, 17

Clinton, Bill, 46, 54

Communications Decency Act (CDA), 46–47, 48, 49, 50, 51

Communists, 27–28, 32

Comstock, Anthony, 19

Comstock Act, 19–21, 48

copyright, 50–51, 105, 106, 108–111, 116–117; digital materials and, 123, 125, 132

Craigslist, 86–87

cyberbullying, 7–12, 70–71

cyberhazards, 64–67, 72

Dalzell, Stewart, 50

Declaration of Independence, 15–16

democracy, 44, 81, 85, 97; free speech and, 12, 88–89, 129; privacy and, 92

Digital Media Consumers' Rights Act (DMCRA), 126–127

Digital Millennium Copyright Act (DMCA), 50–51, 106–108, 112–113, 115, 118–119, 121–127, 132; anti-circumvention provision of, 124–125

Douglas, William O., 34

e-books, 105–106, 122, 123, 125

Economy of Ideas, The, 110–111

ElcomSoft, 105, 106

Electronic Frontier Foundation (EFF), 110, 111, 121
e-mail, 43, 93; spam on, 55–59
Ernst, Morris, 29
espionage. *See* spying
Espionage Act, 22–23, 26, 27

fairness doctrine, 33–34, 40
fair use, 106, 121, 122
Falwell, Jerry, 38–39, 40–41
Family Online Safety Institute, 74–75
Fanning, Shawn, 51
Federal Bureau of Investigation (FBI), 91, 92, 95, 97, 100
Federal Communications Commission (FCC), 33, 79
Feingold, Russ, 102, 103
fighting words, 32–33, 36, 80
file sharing, 51, 114, 120; peer-to-peer, 114–115, 116
filtering software, 47, 52, 55, 56, 67–68, 71, 73, 131
First Amendment, 16–17, 27, 36, 40, 41, 46; text of, 17; value of, 89, 129
Flynt, Larry, 38–39, 40–41
Foreign Intelligence Surveillance Act (FISA), 102, 103
Fourteenth Amendment, 27, 41
Frankfurter, Felix, 35
Franklin, Benjamin, 96
Free Culture, 121–122
freedom of press and media, 18–19, 28–29, 33–34, 38, 40, 44, 89; Internet and, 129–130, 134
freedom of speech, 8–9, 16–18, 43, 85, 129; advocates for, 85, 88; limits on, 17–18, 22–23, 55, 92; value of, 89

gambling, 65
games, online, 74–75

Gates, Bill, 133–134
Geller, Uri, 125–126
Ginsberg v. New York, 35
Gitlow v. New York, 27
global censorship, 101
global security, 98–99
Gonzalez, Alberto R., 69
Google Books, 125
Google Earth, 98–99
Grateful Dead, 110, 111

hackers, 66
hate groups, 82–83, 84–85
Holmes, Oliver Wendell, Jr., 24–25, 36
Holocaust, 36
HR 1966, 7–12
Hustler Magazine Inc. v. Falwell, 38–39, 41

intellectual property, 105–127; computers and, 109–111, 132–133. *See also* copyright
interactive websites, 118–119, 121
Internet, 12, 43, 129–130; age of users, 63; censorship and, 12, 43–59, 101, 130–132, 134–135; child safety and, 45–47, 50, 54–57, 63–75; subnetworks, 133
Internet filters, 47, 52, 55, 56, 67–68, 71, 73, 131
Internet services, most used, 127
iTunes, 114–115, 117

Jackson, Robert, 44
Jefferson, Thomas, 109
Joyce, James, 29–30
JUSTICE Act, 103

law enforcement, 74–75
Lessig, Lawrence, 121

liability protection, 118–119
libraries, 20, 22, 46; Internet and, 52,
    68, 91–92, 100, 107, 125; online, 125
Life magazine, 30–31
Lincoln, Abraham, 18

march on Skokie, 36–37
marketplace of ideas, 36–37, 80–81
media freedoms, 44–45, 46
Megan Meier Cyberbullying Prevention
    Act (HR 1966), 7–12
Miller v. California, 35–36, 37
Minnesota Gag Law, 28–29
morality, 19, 34; public, 78, 80–82,
    83–85
motion pictures, 34, 44, 45, 113, 116
Murphy, Frank, 32–33
music, 114, 115, 120; piracy of, 116–117

Napster, 51, 117
national security, 12, 29, 91–93
national security letters, 91–92, 94–95,
    97
Nazis, 36–37
NetSmartz, 72–73
New York Society for the Suppression
    of Vice, 19
nonverbal speech, 27–28
notice-and-takedown, 118–119, 125

Obama, Barack, 83
obscenity, 17, 29, 30–31, 34–35, 45,
    55, 80, 131; children and, 35; legal
    definition of, 35–36
O'Connor, Kevin, 95–96
offensive speech, 79
Open Book Alliance, 125

parody, 38–39, 40–41
PATRIOT Act, 53–55, 94–95, 100, 103,
    132

peer-to-peer (P2P) sharing, 114–115,
    116
piracy, 106, 114–117, 118
Pirate Bay, 116, 118
Poorman, Yancy, 77–78
pornography, 37; Internet and, 44,
    45–46, 54–57, 68, 71, 80–81, 131;
    sex trafficking and, 84–85
President's Surveillance Program (PSP),
    53, 54–55, 93–94, 100, 103
press and media, freedom of, 18–19,
    28–29, 33–34, 38, 40, 44, 89,
    129–130, 134
privacy, 92–93, 132
Protect Act, 46

racism, 79, 82
Reagan, Ronald, 40
Rehnquist, William, 38
Rotenberg, Marc, 69

Sanchez, Linda, 7, 8
satellites, 98–99
Scalia, Antonin, 56
schools, Internet and, 10–11, 52, 77
Schumer, Charles, 58
Sedition Act, 23, 26, 27
Sekulow, Jay, 57
September 11, 52–53, 93
sex education, 20, 30–31, 55
sex traffickers, 84–85
sexual predators, online, 61–63, 66–67,
    68, 70–71, 74–75
Shaw, George Bernard, 108
Sippel, Rodney, 89
Sklyarov, Dmitry, 105, 106
slavery, 18
Smith Act, 32
social norms, 80–82, 85, 88
Soviet Union, 32
spam, e-mail, 55–59

speech: freedom of, 8–9, 16–18,
    22–23, 43, 55, 85, 88, 89, 92, 129;
    nonverbal, 27–28; symbolic, 36
spying, 22–23, 96–97, 98, 100, 102. *See
    also* Espionage Act
State of the First Amendment, 79
Stevens, John Paul, 47
Stormfront, 82–83
Stromberg, Yetta, 27–28
Supreme Court, 8, 23–24, 27, 29, 32–35,
    40; Internet censorship and, 54–55,
    71, 88
symbolic speech, 36

television, 33–34, 44
terrorism, 13, 52–54, 93; free speech
    and, 93–94; Internet and, 91, 92,
    98–99, 102
torrents, 116–117

Ulysses, 29–30

U.S. Constitution, 16. *See also* First
    Amendment
U.S. Postal Service, 19, 23, 56–57

Viacom, 126
violence, 82, 86
viruses, computer, 56, 57

warrantless wiretapping, 53, 54–55,
    93–94, 96, 102, 132
White, Byron, 44
white supremacy, 82–83
Whitman, Walt, 21
Wilson, Woodrow, 22–23
Wolf, Christopher, 81
World War I, 22–23, 26
World War II, 32–33, 36
World Wide Web, 43–44. *See also*
    Internet

YouTube, 125–126

PHOTO ACKNOWLEDGMENTS

The images in this book are used with the permission of: © Nicholas Kamm/AFP/Getty Images, pp. 4–5; © Jonathan Alcorn/ZUMA Press, p. 6; AP Photo/Tom Gannam, p. 7; National Archives, pp. 14–15, 16; © Bettmann/CORBIS, pp. 19, 28, 38; © Chip East/ Reuters/CORBIS, p. 21; © Lake County Museum/CORBIS, p. 22; Library of Congress, pp. 23(LC-USZ62-20570), 25 (LC-DIG-npcc-26412); © FPG/Getty Images, p. 26; © Lipnitzki/Roger Viollet/Getty Images, p. 30; © Acme/Time & Life Pictures/Getty Images, p. 31; AP Photo, p. 37; AP Photo/Charles Tasnadi, p. 39; © CERN/SSPL/The Image Works, pp. 42–43; © Walter Bennett/Time & Life Pictures/Getty Images, p. 45; AP Photo/Marcy Nighswander, p. 47; AP Photo/Nanine Hartzenbusch, p. 49; AP Photo/ Paul Sakuma, p. 51; AP Photo/Chitose Suzuki, p. 52; © Bob Curtis/Army Times/ USA TODAY, p. 53; AP Photo/Susan Walsh, p. 58; © ColorBlind Images/Getty Images, pp. 60–61, 130; © Anne Ackermann/Digital Vision/Getty Images, p. 64; © Graeme Robertson/Getty Images, p. 65 (bottom); © Scott Barbour/Getty Images, p. 66; © Tim Dillon/USA TODAY, p. 69; AP Photo/Toby Talbot, pp. 76–77; © Cat Gwynn/ CORBIS, p. 80; © Steve Mitchell/USA TODAY, p. 83; © Justin Sullivan/Getty Images, p. 87; © Picture Partners/Alamy, pp. 90–91; © Shawn Thew/AFP/Getty Images, p. 94; © Denny Gainer/USA TODAY, p. 97; AP Photo/Ted S. Warren, p. 100; © sinopictures/ ulstein bild/The Image Works, p. 101; © Darryl Bush/San Francisco Chronicle/CORBIS, pp. 104–105; United States Copyright Office, p. 107; © Ed Kashi/CORBIS, p. 110; Walt Disney/The Kobal Collection, p. 113; PR NewsFoto/Apple, p. 115; © David Brabyn/ CORBIS, p. 118; © Todd Strand/Independent Picture Service, p. 119; © Neilson Barnard/Getty Images, p. 121; AP Photo/Ross D. Franklin, p. 123; © Golden Pixels LLC/ Alamy, pp. 128–129; © USA TODAY, p. 133; © Eileen Blass/USA TODAY, p. 134.

Front cover: © Letterbox Digital/Alamy.

ABOUT THE AUTHOR

Christine Zuchora-Walske is a freelance author and editor. She has written and edited hundreds of nonfiction books for children and parents. Her work for Lerner Publishing Group includes several titles in the Visual Geography and USA TODAY's Debate series. Christine lives in Minneapolis, Minnesota, with her husband and two children.